The Ultimate Gluten and Dairy Free Cookbook

Dr. Cobi Slater, PhD, DNM, RHT, NNCP, RNCP

PhD Natural Health Sciences
Board Certified Doctor of Natural Medicine
Registered Herbal Therapist
Natural Nutritional Consulting Practitioner
Registered Nutritional Consulting Practitioner

Printed in the United States of America.

Cover photo by Donna Milburn of Milburn Photography

Published by Prominence Publishing. For information, visit www.prominencepublishing.com

Dr Cobi Slater can be reached at www.drcobi.com

ISBN: 978-0-9737453-8-2

Acknowledgements

This book is dedicated to all of the people who are struggling with food allergies. May these recipes bring your kitchen back to life!

Thank you to the many people along the way who have helped in the creation of this book.

Thank you to my Mom who is always steadfast in her ongoing support in the way she encourages me and edits my work!

To my sister in law, Heidi Kubin who was alongside me for years in recipe creations and my friend, Natasha Munn who spent countless hours creating menus- I thank you!

Thanks to my family who have been the constant Guinea pigs for my recipes that don't always turn out so well. I have been so blessed to have a family that fully supports the way that our family needs to eat- especially my parents, Terry and Arlene Kubin who not only go the extra mile to keep a well-stocked kitchen with gluten and dairy free foods but have also fully adopted this way of eating!

I thank God for allowing me the privilege of helping people find their way back to delicious tasting food that keeps them healthy and allergy free!

Table of Contents

Introduction

For many of my patients, being diagnosed with food allergies or celiac disease is quite overwhelming. The first question that they often ask is, "What am I going to eat?" As we pour over information and handouts on what to avoid and what is safe, I think to myself, are they going to be able to do it? Do they really understand how important this is to their health?

Several years ago I was in a similar position when both of my sons were diagnosed with celiac disease and multiple food allergies. I was thankful in those moments that I was their Mom. My background in Nutrition and Natural Medicine allowed me to ease through the transition and find all sorts of alternatives to keep my growing boys happy and satisfied. There are moments of frustration and accidental exposure which leads to all sorts of reactions but I would not trade any of it. Why? This journey has allowed me to fully immerse myself with my patients who are going through the same thing. This includes such a wide variety of people from young Moms trying to feed several children to Grandparents trying their best to understand what kind of treats they can give their Grandchildren and everything in between!

This book is a collection of recipes that we rely on as a family for our food. The recipes are easy and delicious and are not only for people with allergies. These recipes can be for anyone who is trying to get healthier, lose weight, lower blood sugar or cholesterol, eliminate inflammation, clear up skin conditions, improve digestion and gain optimal energy.

You will learn how to navigate through a world of food and become an expert in gluten and dairy free cooking. Included is information on how to avoid gluten and dairy as well as the principles of clean eating for abundant health. From my heart to your table, I pray that these recipes are a blessing to you and your family.

Gluten Defined

There are several different types of reactions that can occur with gluten including Celiac disease, IgG, IgA and IgE immune mediated allergies and sensitivities. Celiac disease is the most severe and is a lifelong autoimmune reaction to gluten. 93% of Celiac sufferers carry a genetic marker that predisposes them to Celiac disease. It is estimated that 1 in 100 people have Celiac disease which makes it the most common genetic disease in the world.

In people with Celiac disease, the finger-like villi in the small intestines which normally look like shag carpets are flattened due to an immune system attack. This immune attack causes certain markers to be present in the bloodstream allowing for laboratory screening to verify Celiac disease. The most sensitive and specific tests are tissue transglutaminase and deamidated gliadin antibodies. Positive blood tests usually produce the need to verify the results with a small intestinal biopsy.

There have been over 300 identified symptoms of Celiac disease but some of the most common symptoms of Celiac include:

- Digestive issues such as bloating, vomiting, gas, intestinal pain, diarrhea and irritable bowel
- Weight loss or weight gain
- Chronic headache or migraine
- Chronic anemia
- Skin conditions (dermatitis herpetiformis)
- Joint pain
- Depression or anxiety
- Seizures
- Infertility
- Chronic fatigue
- Failure to thrive (often in children)
- Other autoimmune conditions (Asthma, Hashimotos, Alopecia, Rheumatoid arthritis etc.)

Gluten sensitivity or allergy can trigger the same reactions as Celiac disease but without the autoimmune response and destruction of the small intestinal villi.

Common symptoms of gluten sensitivity include:

- Acne
- ADD or ADHD
- Anxiety or Depression
- Arthritis
- Asthma

- Bedwetting
- Behavioral issues
- Brain fog
- Canker sores
- Cavities
- Chronic infections
- Digestive issues (Diarrhea, constipation, gas, bloating, pain)
- Ear infections
- Eczema or Psoriasis
- Fatigue
- Headaches
- Heartburn
- Hives
- Hormone imbalances
- Insomnia
- Irritable bowel syndrome
- Joint pain
- Nasal congestion

Gluten is the term used for several types of proteins that are commonly found in wheat, barley, rye and some oats. Gluten is made up of the proteins gliadin and glutelin. Gluten is appreciated for its viscoelastic properties. It gives elasticity to dough, helping it rise and keep its shape and often gives the final product a chewy texture.

Gluten is primarily found in foods like bread, pasta, cakes, muffins, crackers and pizza dough. Wheat, barley and rye are used in many baked goods because the gluten allows for elasticity as well as acting as a binding agent. Avoiding gluten can be challenging at first for several reasons. The law does not state that gluten has to be listed on food labels and there is often hidden gluten in foods. The law does however state that the top allergens must be listed on every food label. Wheat is one of the top 8 allergens that must be listed and this is a primary source of gluten. If a label says "contains wheat", you can be sure that it contains gluten. Conversely if the package says “wheat free” that does not necessarily mean that it is "gluten free". There may be a grain that is wheat free but not gluten free in the item such as spelt or kamut. Always choose the product that says "gluten free" to be sure. When in doubt, go without!

The healthiest way to eat gluten free is to choose foods that are naturally gluten free and not man-made gluten free. Try and avoid highly processed gluten free foods such as bagels, muffins, cookies etc. These foods are much higher in starch and sugar than their counterparts. Choose foods such as lean proteins, fresh vegetables and fruits, legumes as well as raw nuts and seeds which are all naturally gluten free.

According to the Celiac Disease Foundation, there are many food items that may contain sources of hidden gluten. Always read the labels of any food products you are buying if gluten-free is not specified on the label.

The following grains and their derivatives are sources of gluten[1]:

(The following information is provided by the Celiac Disease Foundation)

- Wheat
- Varieties and derivatives of wheat such as:
    - wheat starch
    - wheat berries
    - wheat bran
    - wheat germ
    - couscous
    - cracked wheat
    - durum
    - einkorn
    - emmer
    - farina
    - faro
    - fu (common in Asian foods)
    - gliadin
    - graham flour
    - kamut
    - matzo
    - semolina
    - spelt
- Rye
- Barley
- Triticale
- Malt in various forms including malted barley flour, malted milk or milkshakes, malt extract, malt syrup, malt flavoring and malt vinegar
- Oats have no gluten unless processed in plants containing gluten
- Brewer's Yeast
- Wheat Starch that has not been processed to remove the presence of gluten to below 20ppm and adhere to the FDA Labeling Law*

Wheat free products may not be gluten-free. They may contain spelt (a form of wheat), rye or barley-based ingredients containing gluten. Always check the ingredient list!

---

[1] https://celiac.org/live-gluten-free/glutenfreediet/sources-of-gluten/

*According to the FDA requirements for gluten-free labelling, if wheat starch is in a food and labelled gluten-free, by law it contains no more than 20 parts per million of gluten. This makes it safe for people with celiac disease or gluten intolerance. If a product labeled gluten-free contains wheat starch in the ingredient list, it must be followed by an asterisk explaining that the wheat has been processed sufficiently to adhere to the FDA requirements for gluten-free labeling.

Common foods that contain gluten:

- Pastas:
  - raviolis, dumplings, couscous and gnocchi
- Noodles:
  - ramen, udon, soba (those made with only a percentage of buckwheat flour) chow mein and egg noodles. (Note: rice noodles and mung bean noodles are gluten free)
- Breads and Pastries:
  - croissants, pita, naan, bagels, flatbreads, cornbread, potato bread, muffins, donuts, rolls
- Crackers:
  - pretzels, goldfish, graham crackers
- Baked Goods:
  - cakes, cookies, pie crusts, brownies
- Cereal & Granola:
  - corn flakes and rice puffs often contain malt extract/flavoring, granola often made with regular oats, not gluten-free oats
- Breakfast Foods:
  - pancakes, waffles, French toast, crepes and biscuits.
- Breading & Coating Mixes:
  - panko breadcrumbs
- Croutons:
  - stuffings, dressings
- Sauces & Gravies (many use wheat flour as a thickener)
  - traditional soy sauce, cream sauces made with a roux
- Flour tortillas
- Beer (unless explicitly gluten-free) and any malt beverages (see "Distilled Beverages and Vinegars" below for more information on alcoholic beverages)
- Brewer's Yeast
- Anything else that uses "wheat flour" as an ingredient

Foods that may contain gluten (must be verified):

- Energy bars/granola bars – some bars may contain wheat and oats not gluten-free
- French fries – be careful of batter containing wheat flour or cross-contamination from fryers
- Potato chips – some potato chip seasonings may contain malt vinegar or wheat starch

- Processed lunch meats
- Candy and candy bars
- Soup – pay special attention to cream-based soups which have flour as a thickener- many soups also contain barley
- Multi-grain or "artisan" tortilla chips or tortillas that are not entirely corn-based may contain a wheat-based ingredient
- Salad dressings and marinades – may contain malt vinegar, soy sauce or flour
- Starch or dextrin if found on a meat or poultry product could be from any grain including wheat
- Brown rice syrup – may be made with barley enzymes
- Meat substitutes made with seitan (wheat gluten) such as vegetarian burgers, vegetarian sausage, imitation bacon, imitation seafood (Note: tofu is gluten-free, but be cautious of soy sauce marinades and cross-contamination when eating out, especially when the tofu is fried)
- Soy sauce (though tamari made without wheat is gluten-free)
- Self-basting poultry
- Pre-seasoned meats
- Cheesecake filling – some recipes include wheat flour
- Eggs served at restaurants – some restaurants put pancake batter in their scrambled eggs and omelets, but on their own, eggs are naturally gluten-free

Distilled beverages and vinegars

- Vinegars, alcoholic beverages, wines and hard liquor are gluten-free if they are distilled.
- Beers, ales, lagers, malt beverages and malt vinegars are only gluten-free if they are distilled.

Other items that must be verified:

- Lipstick, lip-gloss, and lip balm because they are unintentionally ingested
- Communion wafers
- Herbal or nutritional supplements
- Drugs and over-the-counter medications
- Vitamins & mineral supplements
- Play-dough- avoid wheat based play-dough- make play-dough with gluten-free flour

Cross-Contact

When preparing gluten-free foods, avoid cross-contact with foods or ingredients that come in contact with gluten. Avoid sharing utensils as well as sharing a cooking or storage environment to avoid all contact with gluten.

Places where cross-contact can occur:

- Toasters used for both gluten-free and regular bread
- Colanders
- Cutting boards
- Flour sifters
- Deep fried foods cooked in oil shared with breaded products
- Shared containers including improperly washed containers
- Condiments such as butter, peanut butter, jam, mustard, and mayonnaise may become contaminated when utensils used on gluten-containing food are double-dipped
- Wheat flour can stay airborne for many hours in a bakery (or at home) and contaminate exposed preparation surfaces and utensils or uncovered gluten-free products
- Oats – cross-contact can occur in the field when oats are grown side-by-side with wheat- select only oats specifically labeled gluten-free
- Pizza – pizzerias that offer gluten-free crusts sometimes do not control for cross-contamination with their wheat-based doughs
- French fries
- Non-certified baked goods e.g. “gluten-free” goods from otherwise gluten-containing bakeries
- bulk bins at grocery stores or co-ops

Easily contaminated foods:

- oats must be labelled gluten-free
- pizza with gluten-free crusts cannot be contaminated with wheat-based doughs
- French fries
- non-certified baked goods (e.g. “gluten-free” goods from otherwise gluten-containing bakeries)

All About Dairy

Cows' milk is a staple food for many people, especially children, but it can be the cause of many health problems including digestive disorders, skin conditions, behavioral issues, ear infections, asthma and allergies. This is surprising to many people who believe that milk is natural and health giving. However, when you consider that cows' milk is designed for calves who grow at a much faster rate than babies, and who need to build up particular fermentative bacteria to digest grass, then it becomes easier to see why milk so often causes digestive and other problems in humans.

The enzyme needed to digest milk sugar (lactose) is called lactase and is absent from the adult digestive system of most races except Northern Europeans and their direct descendants. Thus, for most of the world's population, milk is difficult to digest and tends to ferment in the stomach leading to gas and bloating.

Many people are also allergic to the protein found in cows' milk. Children are especially at risk here because in the first year or so of life the lining of the gut is quite leaky and protein particles can enter the blood to set the stage for an allergy reaction either then or later in life. Asthma, eczema and digestive problems are the most common allergic reactions to cows' milk. Goats' milk is often a better alternative as the protein, casein is different in goats' milk that in cow milk.

There are 2 types of reactions to dairy- lactose intolerance and a dairy allergy. Lactose intolerance occurs when the body has the inability to break down the sugar found in the milk of mammals and most commonly in dairy products such as milk, cheese and ice cream. This inability results from a lack of the enzyme, lactase which is responsible for digesting lactose. Deficiencies in lactase prevents the lactose from being broken down into its simpler forms of galactose and glucose before it is absorbed into the intestinal wall. Lactose intolerance affects approximately 70% of the world's population as most people are genetically programmed to decrease the production of lactase after the weaning period. There are varying degrees of lactose intolerance in different ethnic groups. For example, the following percentages show the level of lactose intolerance per ethnic group:

- Native American adults 79%
- Blacks 75%
- Hispanics 51%
- Caucasians 21%

Testing for lactose intolerance can either be done by avoiding lactose containing foods for a period of time followed by a re-introduction to challenge the body to produce symptoms of intolerance. There is also a breath test that can be performed by your Doctor. The test involves drinking a lactose containing beverage and then breathing into a mechanism at regular intervals to detect levels of hydrogen. Undigested lactose produces high levels of hydrogen in the breath.

Symptoms of lactose intolerance usually begin 30 minutes to 2 hours after eating or drinking milk or milk products and can include:

- Bloating
- Abdominal pain or cramps
- Gurgling or rumbling sounds in the lower belly
- Gas
- Loose stools or diarrhea
- Vomiting

A dairy allergy occurs when a person is allergic or intolerant to casein which is the protein found in dairy. A true dairy allergy involves the person needing to avoid all foods that contain casein and this also extends beyond dairy products. It is also not recommended for a person with a dairy allergy to consume lactose free dairy products because they still contain the intact dairy protein, casein.

Symptoms of Dairy Intolerance include:

- Gastro-intestinal issues such as diarrhea, constipation, bloating and Irritable Bowel Syndrome (IBS)
- Depression and/or anxiety
- Weight gain or unexplained weight loss
- Respiratory issues such as coughing, runny nose, excess phlegm production, Asthma, Bronchitis, snoring and Sleep Apnea
- Sinus conditions
- Headache
- Chronic fatigue
- Skin disorders such as Eczema, hives or unexplained rashes
- Decreased immune system which causes ear infections, chronic viruses, Bronchitis and yeast infections (e.g. Thrush)

Severe allergies to casein can be life threatening and can cause symptoms such as:

- Constriction of airways or anaphylaxis reactions
- Facial flushing
- Itching and hives
- Shock and low blood pressure

The following ingredients found on a label indicate the presence of milk protein. All labels should be read carefully before consuming a product:

(The following information was adapted from http://www.kidswithfoodallergies.org/page/milk-allergy.aspx)

- Butter: margarine (often contains casein), artificial butter flavor, butter extract, butter fat, butter flavored oil, butter solids, Ghee, natural butter flavor and whipped butter
- Casein and caseinates: ammonium caseinate, calcium caseinate, hydrolyzed casein, iron caseinate magnesium caseinate, potassium caseinate, sodium caseinate and zinc caseinate
- Cheese: cheese (all types), cheese flavor (artificial and natural), imitation cheese, cheese curds, vegetarian cheeses with casein
- Custard
- Galactose
- Hydrolysates — casein hydrolysate, milk protein hydrolysate, protein hydrolysate, whey hydrolysate, whey protein hydrolysate, Ice cream, ice milk and sherbet
- Lactalbumin and lactalbumin phosphate
- Lactate solids
- Lactitol monohydrate
- Lactoglobulin
- Lactose
- Lactulose
- Lactyc yeast
- Milk: all types of cow, goat or sheep milks including buttermilk, condensed milk, dried milk, dry milk solids (DMS), evaporated milk, lactose free milk, milk derivatives, cream and sweet cream
- Nougat
- Pudding
- Quark
- Rennet and rennet casein
- Sour cream, sour cream solids, imitation sour cream
- Whey — acid whey, cured whey, delactosed whey, demineralized whey, hydrolyzed whey, powdered whey, reduced mineral whey, sweet dairy whey, whey, whey protein, whey protein concentrate, whey powder and whey solids
- Yogurt

The following foods often contain milk:

- "Non-dairy" products (may contain casein)
- Au gratin dishes and white sauces
- Baked goods such as bread, cookies, crackers and cakes

- Caramel flavoring
- Cereals
- Chewing gum, chocolate and cream candy
- Creamed or scalloped foods
- Donuts
- High protein flour
- Malted milk
- Mashed potatoes
- Natural flavoring
- Processed meats including cold cuts, sausages and deli meats
- Rice cheese
- Salad dressings
- Soy cheese

Many people that need to eat dairy free become concerned about their calcium intake. The following information outlines the amount of calcium found in high calcium foods in 100 gram servings:

Sources of Dietary Calcium

Milk Products	**mg/100g**
Cheddar cheese	800
Cow's milk	120
Camembert cheese	380
Yoghurt	180
Cottage cheese	60
Nuts, Seeds and Beans	
Almonds	250
Soy flour	250
Brazil nuts	180
Haricot beans	180
Red kidney beans	140
Tofu	128
Sunflower seeds	120
Buckwheat	114
Sesame seeds	110
Walnuts	61
Peanuts	61
Soy milk	21
Fish	
Whitebait	860
Sardines	550

Shrimp	320
Prawns	150
Haddock	110
Oysters	110
Salmon (canned)	93

Vegetables and Fruit

Parsley	330
Dried figs	280
Turnip greens	250
Kale	225
Watercress	220
Broccoli	100
Apricots (dried)	92

Other

Kelp	1093
Blackstrap molasses	579
Carob powder	352
Brewer's yeast	210

Pantry and Kitchen Items

A well-stocked kitchen is the key to gluten and dairy free living. The following lists will help you to slowly incorporate these items into your pantry, fridge and freezer for all of your cooking needs:

Flours and Baking Needs:

(Gluten free flours are better kept in the freezer as they tend to go rancid quickly-see below for more information of gluten free flours and thickeners)

- Almond flour
- Almond meal
- Amaranth flour
- Arrowroot flour
- Baking Yeast, Nutritional yeast
- Brown rice flour
- Buckwheat flour
- Chick pea flour (garbanzo bean)
- Cocoa powder
- Coconut flour
- Gluten free bread crumbs
- Millet flour
- Potato flour
- Quinoa flour
- Sorghum four
- Tapioca flour
- Teff flour

Standard Staples:

- Balsamic vinegar, Bragg apple cider vinegar, brown rice vinegar
- Beef broth- organic
- Chia seeds
- Chicken broth-organic
- Coconut oil
- Cold pressed extra virgin olive oil
- Dried peas, Lentils and beans (Kidney, pinto, black, cannellini, mung)
- Earth Balance buttery spread
- Flax seed meal or seeds

- Gluten free noodles
- Gluten free peanut butter
- Gluten free rolled oats
- Gluten free soy sauce
- Gluten free steel cut oats
- Gluten free Tamari sauce
- Hemp hearts
- Liquid Coconut Aminos (Soy free coconut sauce)
- Millet
- Milks (Coconut, Almond, Cashew, Rice)
- Nuts (walnuts, cashews, brazil, almonds, pecans, macadamia)
- Quinoa
- Raisins, medjool dates, dried cherries
- Raw Honey
- Red wine vinegar
- Rice (Arborio, Black rice, Brown rice, Jasmine rice, Wild rice)
- Spectrum vegan margarine
- Vegan cheese (Daiya Cheese, Earth Island Coconut Cheese)
- Vegetable broth-organic

Sweeteners and Such:

- Applesauce
- Brown rice syrup
- Enjoy Life Foods chocolate chips (dairy free)
- Black strap Molasses
- Organic cane sugar
- Organic coconut palm sugar
- Organic pure maple syrup
- Pure fruit jams
- Stevia
- Xylitol

Canned Goods:

- Black Beans
- Coconut Milk
- Chick peas
- Rain coast Tuna

- Canned salmon
- Black and green olives
- Diced Tomatoes
- Kidney Beans
- Organic Pumpkin
- Pinto Beans

Herbs and Spices:

- All Spice
- Basil leaves
- Cardamom
- Chili Powder
- Cinnamon
- Crushed Red Pepper Flakes
- Cumin
- Curry powder
- Dill
- Garlic salt
- Ground Cloves
- Ground Ginger
- Himalayan Sea Salt
- Lemon Pepper
- Onion flakes
- Oregano
- Peppercorns
- Tarragon
- Thyme
- Turmeric

Freezer Items:

- Frozen fruit for smoothies (Berries, peaches, mangos, pineapple etc.)
- Gluten-Free Tortillas
- Gluten-Free Bread
- Gluten-Free Hamburger Buns & Hotdog Rolls
- Gluten-Free Pizza Crusts

A Few Notes about Gluten Free Flours and Thickeners

Arrowroot Powder is a starch that can be used in place of cornstarch. It can be used to thicken sauces, gravies or puddings and it can also be used as a starch in a gluten free flour mix.

Bean flours are produced from pulverized beans. These flours provide a great texture and they increase nutritional value as well as protein and fibre without adding much fat. They work well for breads or stronger flavored items like brownies or cookies. You can replace up to ¼ of the amount of wheat flour with bean flour.

Brown rice flour comes from unpolished brown rice. It has more nutritional value than white rice flour because it contains bran which is the outer layers of the grain that contains more nutrients and fibre. This is a versatile flour that can be used in breads, muffins, cookies and cakes.

Buckwheat is gluten free and not related to wheat. It is not even a grain but instead it is related to the rhubarb family. Buckwheat is considered a good source of protein because it contains all of the 8 essential amino acids. The flour has a strong grainy flavor that works well in pancakes, breads and noodles. It can also be used in things like cookies.

Guar gum is a powder that comes from the seed of a legume-like plant. Guar gum is high in soluble fibre, so it can cause digestive upset in some people. Guar gum works well to bind, thicken and to provide texture to gluten- free foods.

Millet flour can help add vitamins and minerals as well as a nice texture to your baked goods. It has a subtle flavor that works well in flour mixes for baked goods.

Nut flours are grated from nuts — most commonly almonds and hazelnuts — and are used in gluten free baking to produce more nutritious and flavorful results. These flours or meals work well in a variety of baked goods from breads to cookies but they work especially well in pastries and pie crusts.

Potato flour is made from ground, dehydrated potatoes. It can be used to thicken soups, gravies or sauces. It also works well in breads, pancakes or waffles.

Potato starch is a fine, white starch that can be used in gluten free baking mixes or as a gluten free thickening agent. Potato starch doesn't have much flavor so it can be used in baking mixes to improve the texture without imparting a strong flavor. It can also be used to thicken sauces or soups.

Quinoa flour is an easy to digest flour which is also high in protein. It can be used with other flours for a variety of baked goods including cookies, breads, brownies or pancakes.

Sorghum flour is a great option for gluten- free baking and cooking. It provides more nutrients than many other gluten- free flour options without imparting a strong flavor. It is a versatile gluten- free flour that can be mixed with other flours and used for a variety of baked goods including cookies, cakes, scones or breads.

Tapioca Flour is a light, white, very smooth starch that comes from the cassava root. It is great for gluten-free baking because it provides a nice chewy texture that is often lacking in gluten- free baked goods. It also works well as a thickener. It can also be used as a starch in a gluten- free flour blend.

White rice flour is milled from polished white rice. It is a good basic flour for gluten free baking because it is light and it doesn't impart any specific flavor to baked goods. White rice flour is pretty versatile and it mixes well with other flours but is low in nutrients.

Xanthan gum is often used as a thickener or stabilizer in foods like sauces and dressings. When it is used for gluten- free cooking, it helps to bind, thicken and to somewhat simulate the texture that gluten provides. It is typically derived from corn, so if you have sensitivities to corn, you may want to avoid it. Xanthan gum works well as a gluten substitute in yeast breads along with other baked goods.

Substitution Solutions

When substituting a recipe for wheat flour to gluten-free flour, the general recommendation is to add approximately ½ to 1 teaspoon of gluten-free flour substitutes depending on what you are making. When making breads and pizza dough, use about 1 teaspoon of gluten substitutes for each cup of gluten-free flour. When making cakes, muffins, quick breads or cookies, use about 1/2 teaspoon of gluten substitutes for each cup of gluten-free flour.

If you are using a gluten-free recipe, then follow the instructions carefully. Too much or too little of gluten free substitutes can cause unfavorable crumbly, heavy or stringy results.

SALADS

Arugula Salad with Lime Vinaigrette

A light and zesty salad. Add a protein like the Caribbean Marinated Chicken to make it a complete meal. Serves 4.

Ingredients

4	cups	arugula leaves (rinsed and drained)
2	cups	mixed greens
1		red bell pepper (sliced into strips)
1		avocado (cubed)
3		green onions (sliced)
1⁄3	cup	sunflower seeds
1⁄4	cup	extra virgin olive oil
1		lime (zested and juiced)
1	tbsp.	apple cider vinegar
1	clove	garlic (minced)
1⁄4	tsp.	sea salt
1	tsp.	cumin
1	pinch	Cardamom

Instructions

1. Place the sunflower seeds, red pepper, avocado and green onion in a salad bowl with the greens.
2. Place remaining ingredients in a small bowl and whisk.
3. Pour the dressing over the salad and serve.

Avocado and Corn Salad

Fresh and delicious, this salad leaves you satisfied. Serve as an accompaniment to Spicy Chicken Lettuce Wraps or a roasted chicken breast for added protein. Serves 4.

Ingredients

1	cup	organic corn kernels
1	can	black beans (rinsed and drained)
2		avocados (diced)
6	cups	salad greens (washed)
3		roma tomatoes (diced)
1/4	cup	cilantro (chopped)
1	clove	garlic (minced)
1	tsp.	cumin
1		lime (juiced)
4	tbsp.	extra virgin olive oil
1/2	tsp.	Himalayan sea salt
1/4	cup	goat feta cheese (crumbled)(optional)

Instructions

1. Divide washed greens evenly among 4 plates.
2. Distribute the corn, beans, avocado, tomato and goat feta, if using, evenly on top of the greens.
3. Whisk together the garlic, cumin, cilantro, lime juice, sea salt and olive oil well.
4. Drizzle dressing over the salad and serve.

Balsamic Salmon Spinach Salad

Healthy, tasty and quick...the perfect combination. Serves 4.

Ingredients

12	oz.	salmon fillet
4	tbsp.	balsamic vinaigrette (divided)
6	cups	spinach
1		avocado (cubed)
2	tbsp.	walnuts (chopped)
2	tbsp.	sunflower seeds
2	tbsp.	dried cranberries
1	cup	cherry tomatoes (halved)

Instructions

1. Brush the salmon with 2 tbsp. of the vinaigrette. Place the salmon on a baking sheet and broil in the oven for 10-15 minutes or until it flakes easily. Divide salmon into 4 pieces.
2. Toss the spinach in a large bowl with the remaining vinaigrette. Divide the spinach among 4 plates and top with the remaining ingredients. Then top with salmon.

Black Bean and Salsa Salad

This dish is totally versatile. It can be used as a salad, side dish or as an appetizer with veggies on the side. Serves 4.

Ingredients

1	can	black beans (drained)
1		orange (juiced)
2		jalapeno peppers (chopped)
1/4	cup	lime juice
1	cup	cilantro (chopped)
1/2	cup	red onion (chopped)
1		red pepper (chopped)
1		green pepper (chopped)
1/2	cup	organic corn (optional)
1		avocado (chopped)

Instructions

1. Mix all ingredients into a large bowl.
2. Cover and refrigerate for 1 hour.

Black-Eyed Pea Salad

A tasty side dish for Coconut Crusted Turkey Strips or Coconut Lime Chicken. Serves 4.

Ingredients

28	oz.	Black-eyed peas (rinsed and drained)
1		green pepper (chopped)
1/2	cup	red onion (chopped)
1	clove	garlic (minced)
1		avocado (cubed)
1/2		lemon (juiced)
1/4	cup	olive oil
3	tbsp.	balsamic vinegar
1	tsp.	organic raw honey

Instructions

1. Toss together black-eyed peas, bell pepper, onion, and garlic in large bowl. Toss avocado with lemon juice in separate bowl. Add avocado to black-eyed pea mixture.
2. Whisk together oil, vinegar, and honey in bowl used for avocado. Add black-eyed pea mixture, and toss to mix.

California Cobb Salad

Everything but the kitchen sink! Serves 4.

Ingredients

8	cups	romaine lettuce (washed and torn)
4	cups	purple cabbage (shredded)
1		cucumber (peeled and chopped)
2		carrots (shredded)
2		eggs (hardboiled and chopped)
1	cup	edamame beans (shelled, cooked and cooled)
4		chicken breasts (cooked and cubed)
½	cup	balsamic vinaigrette
¼	cup	extra virgin olive oil
½	tsp.	dried mustard powder
½	tsp.	pure maple syrup
		Himalayan sea salt and black pepper, to taste

Instructions

1. Toss first 7 ingredients in a large salad bowl.
2. Place next 5 ingredients into a small bowl and whisk until combined.
3. Toss salad with dressing and enjoy this colorful, protein packed salad!

Chicken and Peach Salad

A fresh summer salad you'll love! Serves 4.

Ingredients

3		peaches (peeled and cubed)
2	cups	cooked chicken breasts (cubed)
1		cucumber (seeded and chopped)
3	tbsp.	red onion (finely chopped)
1⁄4	cup	white wine vinegar
1	tbsp.	lemon juice
1⁄3	cup	fresh mint (chopped)
		Himalayan sea salt and black pepper (to taste)
1⁄4	cup	goat cheese (crumbled)(optional)
6	cup	salad greens
1	tbsp.	raw honey

Instructions

1. Combine the peaches, chicken, cucumber and onion in a large bowl and set aside.
2. In a food processor or blender, combine the vinegar, lemon juice, raw honey, mint and salt and pepper. Process until smooth.
3. Drizzle the dressing over the chicken mixture.
4. Divide the salad greens evenly among 4 plates and spoon the chicken mixture over top.
5. Sprinkle the goat cheese, if using, over top and serve.

Chickpea, Artichoke heart and Tomato Salad with Greens

Loaded with protein and fibre, this salad really packs a punch of taste! Serves 4.

Ingredients

1	can	chickpeas (rinsed and drained)
1⁄2	cup	artichoke hearts (rinsed, drained and sliced)
1⁄2	cup	grape tomatoes (halved or quartered)
1⁄3	cup	Kalamata olives (pitted and chopped)
1	cup	fresh parsley (chopped)
4	cups	wild greens
1	oz.	goat feta cheese (crumbled)(optional)
½	cup	balsamic vinaigrette
¼	cup	extra virgin olive oil
½	tsp.	dried oregano
½	tsp.	dried tarragon
½	tsp.	pure maple syrup
		Himalayan sea salt and black pepper, to taste

Instructions

1. Toss together chickpeas, artichoke hearts, tomatoes, olives, and parsley in bowl.
2. Place next 6 ingredients into a small bowl and whisk until combined.
3. Toss chickpea mixture with vinaigrette, then stir in greens and feta, if using.

Curried Chicken Quinoa Salad

High fibre goodness!

Ingredients

2 ½	cups	chicken stock
2	cups	boneless, skinless chicken breast (thinly sliced)
4	tsp.	curry powder (divided)
1	cup	red bell pepper (diced)
1	cup	chickpeas (rinsed and drained)
1⁄2	cup	green onion (chopped)
1⁄2	cup	cilantro
1⁄4	cup	dried cranberries
2	tbsp.	Dijon mustard
6	drops	hot sauce
2	cups	salad greens
3		tomatoes (sliced)
1	cup	quinoa

Instructions

1. In a medium pan, bring the chicken stock to a boil over medium heat.
2. Poach chicken pieces in the stock until cooked through, about 3-5 minutes. Remove to a plate. Toss chicken with 1 ½ teaspoons curry powder and set aside.
3. Return the broth to a boil, add the quinoa and stir. Cover and simmer for 15 minutes. Remove pan from heat and let sit for about 5 minutes.
4. Place quinoa in a mixing bowl and fluff. Stir in the bell pepper, chickpeas, green onion, cilantro and cranberries.
5. Add the Dijon, remaining curry powder and hot sauce and stir until combined.
6. Arrange salad greens and tomato slices on 4 plates and spoon quinoa salad over top.

Fresh Tomato Farfalle with Sweet Corn and Basil

As summer turns to fall the fresh corn and tomatoes are delightful!

Ingredients

¼	cup	lime juice
3	tbsp.	extra virgin olive oil
1	tbsp.	lime zest (grated)
1	tsp.	cumin
5	cups	tomatoes (cut into bite size pieces)
1	can	chick peas (rinsed and drained)
½	cup	fresh basil leaves (torn)
9	oz.	gluten free farfalle pasta (or any small sized gluten free noodle)
1 ¼	cup	fresh corn kernels (frozen can also be used)

Instructions

1. Combine lime juice, lime zest and cumin in a bowl. Add tomatoes, chickpeas and basil; toss to coat. Set aside.
2. Cook pasta according to package directions. Add corn to pasta water 2 minutes before end of cooking time. Drain and toss with tomato mixture. Serve.

Mexicali Chop Chop

This vegetarian salad is bursting with taste. Also makes a great leftover lunch the next day!

Ingredients

1⁄2	cup	extra virgin olive oil
2	cloves	garlic (minced)
2	tsp.	cumin
2	tsp.	coriander
1	tsp.	raw honey
1	tsp.	Himalayan sea salt
1⁄3	cup	lime juice
1⁄4	cup	green onion (chopped)
1⁄4	tsp.	cayenne pepper
8	cups	romaine lettuce (washed and torn)
2	cups	tomatoes (chopped)
1		avocado (diced)
1	cup	celery (chopped)
1		cucumber (seeded and diced)
1	cup	organic corn (fresh or frozen-thawed)
3⁄4	cup	pinto beans
1	cup	red onion (chopped)

Instructions

1. To make Dressing: heat oil, garlic, cumin, coriander, honey and sea salt in saucepan 2 to 3 minutes over low heat, or until garlic begins to sizzle.
2. Blend lime juice, green onion and cayenne pepper with garlic oil in blender until smooth.
3. Toss together all salad ingredients with salad dressing and divide among 4 plates.

Potato Taco Salad

The potatoes give this old favourite a unique twist.

Ingredients

1	clove	garlic (minced)
1	tsp.	cumin (divided)
1		lime (juiced)
1	tsp.	chili powder (divided)
1/2	c	dairy free coconut yogurt or soaked cashews (see note)
1	lb.	nugget potatoes (boiled and cooled)
1	tsp.	extra virgin olive oil
8	cups	mixed wild greens
1		avocado (diced)
1/2	cup	black olives (sliced)
1		tomato (diced)
1	cup	black beans (drained and rinsed)
1/2	cup	red bell pepper (chopped)
2	tbsp.	fresh cilantro (torn)

Instructions

If using soaked cashews to replace yoghurt - simply soak ½ cup raw cashews in cold water for 2 hours minimum or overnight. Drain and rinse thoroughly. Blend with ½ cup water, a dash of sea salt.

For dressing:

1. Whisk first 5 ingredients together. Set aside

For salad:

1. Dice cooled potatoes.
2. Heat olive oil in non-stick skillet. Place potatoes and dressing in skillet. Cook until heated through and crispy around edges.
3. Arrange greens on plates and divide potatoes and the rest of the ingredients as desired.

Curried Quinoa

Dried cranberries and just a touch of curry gives this quick side dish a kick of flavor. This is a great way to use up leftover quinoa and is great on its own or as an accompaniment.

Ingredients

1	cup	quinoa
2	cups	water
1	tsp.	curry powder
4		green onions (diced)
1⁄4	cup	dried cranberries
1⁄4	cup	walnuts (chopped)

Instructions

1. In a medium pot, bring 2 cups of water to boil. Add quinoa, cover and simmer on medium heat until the water is absorbed, about 15 minutes.
2. Stir in the rest of the ingredients and serve.

Green Quinoa Salad

Serve on its own or is great when paired with either Honey Lime Chicken Breasts or Lemon Marinated Flank Steak.

Ingredients

1	cup	quinoa
2	cups	water
1	cup	chickpeas (rinsed and drained)
3		green onion (chopped)
1/2	cup	carrots (shredded)
1/2	tsp.	cumin
1	tbsp.	curry powder
2	cups	spinach (chopped)
1/2	tsp.	Himalayan sea salt

Instructions

1. Boil 2 cups of water in a medium pot. Add the quinoa, cover and simmer for 15 minutes.
2. Once the quinoa is cooked, stir in the remaining ingredients and serve.

Quinoa and Apple Salad

A twist on the well-loved classic Waldorf Salad. This is great as leftovers for lunch the next day.

Ingredients

1 1⁄2	cups	red quinoa
3	cups	water
4	tbsp.	extra virgin olive oil
1		red onion (quartered and thinly sliced)
2	tbsp.	balsamic vinegar
3	cups	arugula (thinly sliced)
1⁄2	cup	goat cheese (crumbled)(optional)
3		celery stalks (thinly sliced)
1		apple (diced)
1⁄2	cup	walnuts (chopped)
1	cup	fennel (diced)
1⁄2	cup	dried cranberries
3	tbsp.	cider vinegar

Instructions

1. Boil 3 cups water in a pot. Add the quinoa, cover, reduce heat and simmer for about 15 minutes or until quinoa is tender and water has been absorbed.
2. While the quinoa is cooking, heat 2 tbsp. olive oil in a nonstick skillet and add the onion. Cook for about 5 minutes or until tender. Add the balsamic vinegar and toss with the onions.
3. Mix the quinoa, onion, arugula, feta, if using, celery, apple, walnuts, fennel and cranberries in a large bowl.
4. In a small bowl, mix the remaining olive oil and cider vinegar with a whisk.
5. Add this dressing to the quinoa mixture and toss to coat. You may add more olive oil if needed.

Quinoa and Avocado Salad

Red quinoa can be found in most grocery stores in the bulk section; however white quinoa can also be used for this recipe. The dried fruit and sweet paprika give this salad a unique kick.

Ingredients

3	tbsp.	raisins
2	tbsp.	dried apricots (thinly sliced)
1	cup	red quinoa
2	cups	water
1		lemon (zested and juiced)
2	tbsp.	extra virgin olive oil
1/2	tsp.	ground coriander
1/2	tsp.	cumin
1/2	tsp.	sweet paprika
2		avocados (peeled and cut into small chunks)
2		green onions (thinly sliced)
1		carrot (peeled and grated)
2	tbsp.	almonds (chopped)

Instructions

1. Soak the raisin and apricots in hot water for 5 minutes in a medium bowl. Drain and set aside.
2. Bring 2 cups of water and the quinoa to boil over medium heat. Cover, reduce the heat and simmer until the water is absorbed and the quinoa is tender. When done, fluff with a fork and let cool.
3. In a small bowl, mix the lemon zest and 1 tbsp. lemon juice with the olive oil, coriander, cumin, paprika and 1/4 tsp salt.
4. In a large bowl, toss the above vinaigrette with the quinoa, raisins, apricots, avocado, carrot, green onion and almonds. Serve.

Quinoa and Spinach Salad

A mix of textures and tastes creates this delicious side salad. Pair this with Greek Fish Filets for a delightful combination. Serves 4.

Ingredients

1	cup	quinoa
6	cups	spinach (torn)
1/2	cup	dried cranberries
3	tbsp.	extra virgin olive oil
1		orange (juiced)
1	tbsp.	red wine vinegar
1	tbsp.	pure maple syrup
1	clove	garlic (minced)
1/2	tsp.	sea salt
1/8	tsp.	pepper
2		green onions (chopped)
1/4	cup	pecans

Instructions

1. Bring 2 cups water to a boil in a small saucepan. Add the quinoa, reduce heat, cover and simmer for about 15 minutes or until the water is absorbed. Let stand to cool.
2. Combine the quinoa, spinach and cranberries in a large bowl.
3. In a small bowl, whisk together the oil, orange juice, vinegar, syrup, garlic, salt and pepper. Stir in the green onion. Pour this over the spinach and quinoa mixture. Toss to coat.
4. Sprinkle with pecans and serve.

Roasted Beets with Orange Slices

Can't "beet" this side dish! Serve with Moroccan Chicken Skewers.

Ingredients

4		beets (trimmed and scrubbed)
2		oranges
2	tbsp.	lemon juice
1/2	tsp.	Himalayan sea salt
2	tbsp.	extra virgin olive oil
1	tbsp.	red wine vinegar

Instructions

1. Preheat oven to 400°F. Wrap each unpeeled beet individually in foil. Place on baking sheet, and roast 40 minutes, or until beets are tender enough to be pierced with knife. Cool until easy to handle.
2. Grate 1/2 tsp. zest from 1 orange; set zest aside. Remove the remaining peel from oranges and cut into segments.
3. Squeeze 2 tbsp. orange juice into bowl and add vinegar, orange zest, lemon juice, and salt. Gradually whisk in oil.
4. Peel beets by rubbing off skin under cold running water. Cut beets into 1-inch pieces and add to bowl with orange segments. Top with vinaigrette and toss well. Chill several hours or up to 2 days prior to serving.

Santa Fe Beef Salad

A quick and delicious salad that is packed with protein. Use leftover steak for a quick dinner.

Ingredients

2	tsp.	extra virgin olive oil
1	lb.	flank steak
1/4	tsp.	Himalayan sea salt
1/4	tsp.	black pepper
8	cups	salad greens
4		ripe plum tomatoes (sliced)
1	can	black beans (rinsed)
1		avocado (sliced)
1/2	cup	dairy free coconut yogurt or soaked cashews (see note)
1		lime (juiced)
1	clove	garlic (minced)
1	tsp.	chili powder
1	tsp.	cumin

Instructions

If using soaked cashews to replace yoghurt- simply soak ½ cup raw cashews in cold water for 2 hours minimum or overnight. Drain and rinse thoroughly. Blend with ½ cup water, a dash of sea salt.

1. Sprinkle beef with salt and pepper. Grill steak on each side for about 10 minutes or until desired doneness. Remove from grill and thinly slice diagonally across the grain.
2. Evenly divide salad greens among plates. Place steak, tomatoes, black beans and avocado on top of salad greens.
3. Combine the yogurt, lime juice, garlic, chili powder and cumin in a small bowl and whisk to combine.
4. Drizzle dressing over the salad and serve.

Shrimp and Vegetable Salad

A light, yet filling warm veggie and crunchy green salad for a midweek meal.

Ingredients

6	cups	salad greens
1/4	cup	extra virgin olive oil (divided)
2	cloves	garlic (minced)
2	tsp.	ginger (chopped)
1/2		red onion (thinly sliced)
1	cup	shiitake mushrooms (sliced)
1		red bell pepper (julienned)
1/2	cup	snow peas (trimmed)
24		jumbo shrimp (peeled and deveined)
2	tbsp.	rice vinegar
1		orange (zested and juiced)
1	tbsp.	sweet chili sauce
3	tsp.	cilantro (chopped)
2	tsp.	gluten free tamari

Instructions

1. Divide the salad greens among 4 plates and set aside.
2. In a large nonstick skillet sauté 1 tbsp. olive oil over medium heat. Add the garlic and ginger and sauté for about 15 seconds.
3. Add the onion, mushrooms, red pepper and snow peas and sauté for another 3 minutes.
4. Add the shrimp and sauté until they begin to turn pink and then add the vinegar, orange zest and orange juice.
5. Toss in the remaining 3 tbsp. olive oil, the chili sauce, cilantro and tamari and stir to combine. Place the shrimp and vegetables over the greens and drizzle the dressing over top.

Side Salad

Throw this together to complement any meal!

Ingredients

3	cups	mixed greens
1	cup	goat cheese (crumbled)(optional)
¼	cup	pecans (chopped)
¼	cup	pumpkin seeds
¼	cup	dried cranberries
		balsamic vinaigrette (to coat)

Instructions

1. Toss first 5 ingredients in a bowl to combine.
2. Drizzle vinaigrette dressing over salad and toss to coat.

Sizzling Sesame Chicken Salad

Use leftover chicken for a real time saver!

Ingredients

2	tsp.	sesame seeds
12	oz.	boneless chicken breasts (approx. 3 breasts)
1/2	tsp.	Himalayan sea salt
1/2	tsp.	black pepper
2	tsp.	extra virgin olive oil
1	cup	celery (diced)
1	cup	bean sprouts
1	cup	carrot (shredded)
1/2	cup	green onion (divided)
1	tbsp.	ginger root (minced)
2	tsp.	raw honey
2	tsp.	gluten free tamari
1/2	tsp.	red pepper flakes
4	cups	salad greens

Instructions

1. Season chicken with salt and pepper. Sauté chicken in olive oil over medium heat until cooked through. Let cool and dice.
2. Combine the chicken, celery, sprouts, carrot, half of the green onion, ginger root, honey, tamari, pepper flakes and sesame seeds. Mix well.
3. Place 1 cup of salad greens on each plate and top with the chicken mixture. Sprinkle remaining green onion on top.

Southwest Grilled Chicken Salad

Packed with nutrients and flavour, this salad is sure to satisfy. The hint of cumin and chili combined with the slight sweetness of raw honey gives this a pleasant Mexican flavour.

Ingredients

2		boneless, skinless chicken breasts
1/2	tbsp.	chili powder
1/2	tsp.	ground coriander
1/2	tsp.	cumin
5	tbsp.	extra virgin olive oil (divided)
2		limes (juiced)
2	tbsp.	cilantro (chopped and divided)
1	cup	black beans (rinsed and drained)
1	cup	cherry tomatoes (halved)
2		green onion (thinly sliced)
8	cups	salad greens
1		avocado (sliced)
1	tsp.	raw honey

Instructions

1. Preheat the grill. Combine the chili powder, coriander, cumin and 1/2 tsp salt in a small bowl. Rub all over both sides of the chicken breasts and let it sit while the grill heats.
2. Grill the chicken on each side until it is no longer pink inside. Remove from the grill and let it cool off. Once cool, thinly slice it.
3. In a small container with a lid, combine the olive oil, lime juice, 1 tbsp. of the cilantro and honey. Shake well to combine.
4. Mix the black beans, tomatoes, green onion and remaining cilantro in a bowl. Add 2 tbsp. of the dressing and gently toss.
5. Place the greens in a bowl and toss with the dressing to lightly coat.
6. Arrange the greens on four plates. Place the chicken, avocado and bean mixture over the greens and sprinkle with cilantro leaves.

Turkey Salad

A tarragon mustard vinaigrette completes this tasty salad

Ingredients

1 1⁄2	cups	turkey breast (cut into 1/2 inch cubes)
1	cup	celery (thinly sliced)
1⁄3	cup	almonds (sliced)
1		apple (diced into 1/2 inch cubes)
1⁄3	cup	goat cheese (optional)
6	cups	romaine lettuce (torn into bite size pieces)
2	tsp.	fresh tarragon (chopped)
2	tsp.	grainy Dijon mustard
2	tbsp.	white wine vinegar
4	tbsp.	extra virgin olive oil
		Himalayan salt and pepper (to taste)

Instructions

1. Toss the turkey, celery, almonds and apple together in a large bowl. Add the goat cheese, if using.
2. Whisk together the tarragon, mustard, vinegar, olive oil and salt and pepper in a small bowl.
3. Pour the vinaigrette over the turkey mixture and toss well.
4. Divide the lettuce evenly among 4 plates and spoon the turkey mixture on top.

SOUPS & STEWS

African Peanut Soup

A delicious soup brimming with warmth and exotic tastes.

Ingredients

1	tbsp.	extra virgin olive oil
1		onion (chopped)
3	cloves	garlic (minced)
1	tbsp.	ginger (minced)
1 1/2	tsp.	cumin
1 1/2	tsp.	coriander
1/2		cinnamon stick
1	pinch	ground cloves
3		tomatoes (chopped)
2		sweet potatoes (peeled and chopped)
1		carrot (peeled and chopped)
1	tsp.	sea salt
1/4	cup	dry roasted peanuts
2	tbsp.	organic peanut butter
1	can	chickpeas (drained and rinsed)
1/4	cup	cilantro (chopped)

Instructions

1. Heat oil in a large saucepan over medium-high heat.
2. Add the onion and cook, stirring frequently, about 3 to 4 minutes.
3. Stir in garlic, ginger, cumin, ground coriander, cinnamon stick, and a pinch of ground cloves. Cook for 3 minutes, stirring frequently.
4. Add the tomatoes, sweet potatoes, and carrot to the onion mixture and cook for 5 minutes, stirring occasionally.
5. Stir in 5 cups water and salt. Bring the mixture to a boil, reduce heat, cover, and simmer for 30 minutes or until the sweet potatoes and carrots are tender.
6. Remove soup from heat and cool. Remove the cinnamon stick.
7. Using a hand blender or food processor, blend the soup. Return the soup to the pot and stir in a pinch of cayenne pepper, the peanuts and peanut butter. Whisk until the peanut butter is completely combined with the soup.
8. Stir chickpeas into the soup, reheat and season with salt and pepper.
9. Garnish with cilantro.

Beet Borscht

Nothing "beets" a bowl of borscht!

Ingredients

4		beets (with greens)
1	tbsp.	extra virgin olive oil
2		carrots (chopped)
2		onions (chopped)
1	lb.	tomatoes (crushed)
4	cups	vegetable broth
1	tbsp.	lemon juice
1	tbsp.	balsamic vinegar
1	tbsp.	fresh dill
1⁄2	tsp.	salt

Instructions

1. Wash the beets and cut of the greens. Chop greens and set aside.
2. Slice the beets and boil for 25-30 minutes. Cool and cut into cubes. Set aside.
3. Heat the oil in a large pot over medium heat and sauté the carrots and onions until soft.
4. Add the beet greens and cook until wilted. Add tomatoes, cover and simmer for 5 minutes.
5. Add vegetable broth, cover and simmer for another 20 minutes.
6. Add beets, lemon juice, vinegar, dill salt and a dash of pepper. Heat through and serve.

Cashew Chicken Stew

Cashew butter gives this a fantastic nutty flavor

Ingredients

2	cups	red onion (chopped)
1		red bell pepper (sliced)
1⁄2	tsp.	black pepper
3	cups	chicken stock
1	lb.	boneless, skinless chicken breasts (cubed)
4	tbsp.	parsley (chopped)
1		apple (cubed)
1	cup	chickpeas (rinsed and drained)
1⁄2	tsp.	sea salt
1⁄4	cup	cayenne pepper
1⁄2	cup	cashew butter

Instructions

1. Sauté onions, red pepper and half of the black pepper in a nonstick skillet until onion is soft.
2. Add the vegetable stock, chicken and parsley and bring to a boil. Simmer until chicken is cooked through.
3. Add the apple, peas, salt, cayenne pepper and remaining black pepper to the pot. Cover and simmer for 10 minutes. Whisk in cashew butter until blended. Serve.

Cashew Stew

A delicious warming stew packed full of protein and essential fatty acids.

Ingredients

1⁄2	cup	cashew butter (unsalted; finely ground raw cashews could also be used)
1	cup	red onion (diced)
1		red pepper (sliced into strips)
3	cups	low sodium chicken broth
1	cup	lima beans (frozen)
1	lb.	chicken breast (cubed)
1⁄4	cup	parsley (fresh or 2 tbsp. dried)
1		Granny smith apple (cored and cubed)
1⁄4	tsp.	cayenne pepper
		Himalayan sea salt and pepper (to taste)

Instructions

1. In a large nonstick pan, sauté onions and red pepper for 5 minutes.
2. Add broth, chicken and parsley. Cover and bring to a boil. Simmer until chicken is cooked through and remove from pot.
3. Add apple, lima beans, salt and pepper, cayenne pepper to broth. Cover and simmer for 10 minutes. Uncover and whisk in cashew butter until well blended. Return chicken to pot and serve.

Chicken and Cauliflower Soup

Curry powder and coconut milk give this soup a tasty Indian flair.

Ingredients

1⁄4	cup	coconut milk
3		boneless, skinless chicken breast (cubed)
4	tsp.	curry powder
4	cups	cauliflower (chopped)
1		red bell pepper (chopped)
1		red potato (unpeeled and chopped)
4	cups	chicken stock
		Himalayan sea salt and pepper
2		green onion (chopped)
1⁄2	cup	cilantro (chopped)

Instructions

1. Place coconut milk in a large pot and heat, being careful not to boil. Add chicken and curry powder. Cook until chicken is golden.
2. Add cauliflower, bell pepper, potato and stock, bring to a boil, cover and reduce heat. Simmer for 10 minutes.
3. Uncover, cook a couple more minutes until vegetables are tender and soup begins to thicken.
4. Sprinkle with green onions and cilantro.

Hamburger Soup

This is my Dad's famous Hamburger Soup. He loves making soup for people who need a little love. This is sure to warm the soul of anyone who eats it.

Ingredients

2	tbsp.	extra virgin olive oil
1		onion (finely chopped)
2		carrots (sliced)
1	clove	garlic (minced)
1		green bell pepper (chopped)
2		celery stalks (sliced)
1	lb.	organic ground beef (or bison, venison)
1/2	tsp.	dried basil
1/2	tsp.	dried oregano
1/2	tsp.	dried rosemary
1/2	tsp.	onion powder
1/2	tsp.	sea salt
4	cups	organic beef stock

Instructions

1. Heat the oil in a large pot over medium heat. Add the garlic, onion, carrots, pepper and celery. Stir until the vegetables begin to soften.
2. Add the beef and cook until the meat is no longer pink.
3. Add the seasonings and cook for another minute.
4. Add the beef stock and bring to a boil.
5. Reduce the heat and simmer for about 10 minutes.
6. Alternatively, brown the meat and then add all ingredients can be added to the crockpot and cooked on low for 8 hours.

Harvest Soup

Throw it all in a pot and enjoy this tasty soup.

Ingredients

8	cups	chicken stock
1		onion (chopped)
2		carrots (peeled and chopped)
1		rotisserie chicken
4		celery ribs (chopped)
2		green apples
2		sweet potatoes
2	tbsp.	extra virgin olive oil
1	tsp.	Himalayan sea salt
½	tsp.	ground black pepper
1/2	cup	apple cider vinegar
1	tsp.	dried basil
1	tsp.	dried parsley

Instructions

1. Place chicken stock in a large pot and heat over medium heat.
2. Add pieces of chicken from rotisserie chicken and reduce heat, simmer on low.
3. In a medium pan, heat olive oil over medium heat. Add all chopped vegetables and cook until soft.
4. Add apples and continue to cook, stirring frequently. When vegetables and apple are cooked, add to stock.
5. Add remaining spices, salt and cider and boil. Reduce heat and let simmer for 20 minutes.
6. Alternatively, add all ingredients to crock pot and cook on low for 6 hours.

Lasagna Soup

A meal time favourite in a bowl...

You may substitute the ground bison with beef or venison.

Ingredients

1	lb.	ground bison
1		green bell pepper (chopped)
1		onion (chopped)
2	cloves	garlic (minced)
3 1/2	cups	organic beef stock
2	can	diced tomatoes (14 oz. each)
1	cup	tomato sauce
1	cup	organic frozen corn
1/4	cup	tomato paste
2	tsp.	Italian seasoning
1/4	tsp.	black pepper
1	cup	gluten free rotini noodles

Instructions

1. Cook bison, green pepper, onion and garlic in a large saucepan and heat over medium heat until meat is no longer pink. Drain.
2. Stir in the broth, tomatoes, tomato sauce, corn, tomato paste, Italian seasoning and pepper.
3. Bring to a boil and stir in the pasta. Simmer for 10-12 minutes or until pasta is tender.

Lentil Sausage Soup

The combination of lentils and sausage makes this a hearty meal the whole family will love.

Ingredients

1	tbsp.	extra virgin olive oil
1		onion (diced)
2		carrots (diced)
2		celery stalks (chopped)
4	cups	chicken stock
4	cups	water
1	can	crushed tomatoes
2	cloves	garlic (minced)
1	lb.	dry lentils (rinsed and drained)
2		bay leaves
1/2	lb.	turkey sausage (sliced)

Instructions

1. In a large pot, heat oil over medium heat.
2. Add the onions, carrots and celery to the pot and cook for 2-3 minutes.
3. Add sausage, chicken stock, 4 cups water, tomatoes, garlic, lentils and bay leaves to the pot and bring to a boil. Reduce heat and simmer for an hour and a half. Season with salt and pepper.
4. Alternatively place all ingredients in crock pot and cook on low for 8 hours.

Lovely Lentil Soup

The crock pot is my best friend during the week. At least 1-2 times per week I fill it with delicious ingredients and come home at the end of a long day to a fully cooked meal - bliss!

Ingredients

2	tbsp.	extra virgin olive oil
1		sweet potato (peeled and chopped)
1		onion (diced)
4	cloves	garlic (minced)
1	tbsp.	curry powder
1	tsp.	cinnamon
1	tsp.	sea salt
1	cup	dry red lentils (rinsed)
4	cups	vegetable stock
2	tbsp.	tomato paste
1 1⁄2	tbsp.	ginger root (peeled and minced)

Instructions

1. In a large pot, heat the olive oil over medium heat.
2. Add the sweet potato, onion, ginger and garlic and cook until softened.
3. Stir in the curry powder, cinnamon and sea salt. Cook for 2-3 minutes longer.
4. Add the lentils, vegetable stock and tomato paste and stir well.
5. Bring to a boil, reduce heat and simmer for 30 minutes or until lentils are cooked.
6. Remove from heat and serve.
7. Alternatively put all ingredients into crockpot and cook on low for 8 hours.

Mexican Chicken Stew

A delicious meal from South of the Border.

Ingredients

1	lb.	boneless, skinless chicken breast (cut to bite size chunks)
2	tsp	extra virgin olive oil
1	lb.	sweet potato (peeled and cut into bite sized chunks)
1		yellow bell pepper (cut into bite size chunks)
1	cup	onion (chopped)
1	can	diced tomatoes
2	tbsp.	chili powder
2	cloves	garlic (minced)
1	tsp.	dried oregano
1	can	corn
1	can	kidney beans (rinsed)
1⁄2	cup	cilantro (chopped coarsely)
1 1⁄2	tbsp.	gluten free flour

Instructions

1. Sprinkle chicken with gluten flour and toss to coat. Heat olive oil in large pot and add chicken. Cook for 5 minutes or until cooked through.
2. Add sweet potatoes, yellow pepper and onion and cook until lightly colored.
3. Add 2 cups water, tomatoes, chili powder, garlic and oregano. Reduce heat, cover and simmer until vegetables are almost tender, about 10 minutes.
4. Add corn and beans, simmer for 5 minutes.
5. Remove from heat and stir in cilantro.

Minestrone Soup

A gluten free version of a classic recipe.

Ingredients

3	tbsp.	extra virgin olive oil
1	cup	onion (chopped)
1⁄2	cup	zucchini (chopped)
1⁄2	cup	green beans
1		celery stalk (chopped)
4	cloves	garlic (minced)
4	cups	vegetable broth
2	can	kidney beans (drained)
2	can	small white beans
1	can	diced tomatoes
1⁄2	cup	carrot (shredded)
2	tbsp.	parsley (minced)
1 1⁄2	tsp.	oregano
1 1⁄2	tsp.	Himalayan sea salt
1⁄2	tsp.	black pepper
1⁄2	tsp.	dried basil
1⁄2	tsp.	dried thyme
4	cups	fresh spinach
1	cup	gluten free pasta shells

Instructions

1. Heat oil in a large soup pot over medium heat. Sauté onion, celery, garlic, green beans and zucchini for about 5 minutes.
2. Add broth, drained tomatoes, kidney and white beans, carrots, 3 cups water and herbs to the pot.
3. Bring to a boil, reduce heat and simmer for about 20 minutes.
4. Add spinach and pasta and cook for another 20 minutes.

Sausage and Vegetable Soup

Lots of veggies, little bit of sausage...a fantastic one pot combination!

Ingredients

1		onion (chopped)
1	cup	zucchini (finely chopped)
1/2	cup	carrots (finely chopped)
1/2	cup	celery (finely chopped)
1/2	tsp.	sea salt (divided)
3	cloves	garlic (minced)
2	tbsp.	tomato paste
1/4	tsp.	red pepper flakes
3	cups	chicken stock (divided)
2	can	cannellini beans (rinsed and drained)
1	tsp.	dried rosemary
1/2	tsp.	black pepper
4	oz.	chicken or turkey Italian sausage

Instructions

1. Break sausage up into pieces and place in a large pot over medium heat. Cook until browned, about 4 minutes. Remove sausage from pan and set aside.
2. Add onion, zucchini, carrots, celery, 1/4 tsp salt and garlic to pot and cook until vegetables are tender.
3. Stir in tomato paste and red pepper flakes and cook for 1 minute.
4. Place 1 cup of the vegetable mixture, 1/2 cup chicken stock and 1 can of beans in a food processor and pulse until smooth.
5. Place pureed bean mixture back in the pot and add remaining broth and the other can of the beans. Bring to a boil, reduce heat and simmer for 20 minutes.
6. Remove from heat and stir in remaining 1/4 tsp salt, rosemary and black pepper.

Spiced Up Chicken Soup

A delicious Mexican inspired soup for a cold night.

Ingredients

2 1/2	tsp.	chili powder
2	tsp.	cumin
1 1/2	tsp.	ground coriander
1	tsp.	dried oregano
1	tsp.	black pepper
1/2	tsp.	Himalayan sea salt
1	tbsp.	extra virgin olive oil (divided)
1	lb.	boneless, skinless chicken breasts (cut into strips)
1 1/2	cups	red onion (chopped)
1	cup	red bell pepper
1	cup	green bell pepper
1	cup	yellow bell pepper
2	cloves	garlic (minced)
2	cups	organic corn kernels
4	cups	chicken stock
28	oz.	crushed tomatoes
2	tbsp.	lime juice

Instructions

1. Combine the first 6 ingredients in a small bowl to prepare the spice blend. Set aside.
2. In a large saucepan, heat 2 tsp oil and add chicken and 1 1/2 tbsp. spice blend. Sauté for about 8 minutes or until done.
3. Chop chicken and set aside.
4. Heat remaining 1 tsp oil in a pan over medium heat and sauté onion, bell peppers, garlic, 1/2 tsp salt and remaining spice blend.
5. Sauté until vegetables are tender. Stir in chicken, corn, chicken stock and tomatoes. Boil, reduce heat and simmer for 15 minutes.
6. Add lime juice and serve.

Sweet Potato and Chorizo Soup

The creamy, smooth texture of the sweet potatoes, combined with the spicy chorizo sausage makes this a stand out soup.

Ingredients

2		carrots (peeled and sliced)
2		celery stalks (sliced)
2		onions (chopped)
2	cloves	garlic (minced)
1 1⁄2	lb.	sweet potatoes (peeled and chopped)
8	oz.	chorizo sausage (cooked and sliced)
1	cup	parsley (finely chopped)
8	cups	vegetable broth
2	tbsp.	extra virgin olive oil
1	tsp	curry powder

Instructions

1. In a large pot, add the broth and bring to a boil.
2. Meanwhile, heat a large pan with olive oil and add remaining ingredients, except sausage.
3. Cook for about 10 minutes or until the onion is lightly browned.
4. Add the vegetables to the broth.
5. Reduce heat and simmer for about 10 minutes, or until the potato is cooked through.
6. Using an immersion blender or food processor, pulse the soup until smooth.
7. Add sausage, season with salt and pepper and serve.

Thai Chicken Soup

For a grain free option substitute spiralized zucchini for soba noodles. Either use a vegetable spiralizer or vegetable peeler to form zucchini into noodles.

Ingredients

2		large boneless, skinless chicken breasts (sliced into 1/4 inch strips)
2	tbsp.	gluten free tamari sauce
1	tsp.	fresh ginger (minced)
1	clove	garlic (minced)
2	tbsp.	rice wine vinegar
2	tbsp.	sesame oil
4	cups	low sodium chicken broth
1⁄2	cup	frozen peas
2	cups	broccoli (chopped)
1⁄4	cup	red pepper (sliced)
1		carrot (peeled and grated)
4		green onions (sliced on the diagonal)
4	cups	spinach (chopped)
1⁄4	cup	roasted peanuts (chopped (optional))
8	oz.	gluten free soba noodles (sub spiralized zucchini for a grain free option)

Instructions

1. Combine chicken, tamari, ginger, garlic, rice wine vinegar and toasted sesame oil in a small saucepan. Heat on medium heat.
2. Add broth and bring to a gentle boil. Continue cooking until chicken is no longer pink – about 10 minutes.
3. Add noodles (if using zucchini noodles, do not add until the very end), peas, broccoli and red pepper. Cook until broccoli is tender-crisp. Reduce heat and let sit, covered.
4. Add carrot and green onion.
5. When ready to serve, divide spinach leaves among bowls at the bottom of each bowl. Add zucchini noodles, if using. Ladle soup into each bowl, making sure to divide ingredients as evenly as possible. Garnish with peanuts (if using).

Tuscan White Bean Soup

Nothing beats a warm bowl of soup on a cool night.

Ingredients

1	tbsp.	extra virgin olive oil
1		scallion (chopped)
1		red onion (chopped)
1		red pepper (chopped)
1		yellow pepper (chopped)
2	cloves	garlic (minced)
1⁄4	cup	dried Italian herbs
15	oz.	canned diced tomatoes
8	cups	vegetable broth
2	cups	water
1⁄4	cup	brown rice
3	cups	spinach leaves (chopped)
1⁄4	tsp.	Himalayan sea salt and black pepper

Instructions

1. Heat olive oil in soup pot over medium heat. Sauté the scallion, onion, peppers and garlic until the onion is lightly browned. Add the Italian herbs and tomatoes and continue to cook for 2 minutes, stirring constantly.
2. Add broth, water, beans and rice and bring soup to a boil. Reduce heat to medium-low and simmer for 45 minutes.
3. Stir in the spinach and continue simmering for 10-15 minutes. Season with salt and pepper.

White Bean Stew

Packed with protein and veggies and so easy to make.

Ingredients

1		yellow bell pepper (cut in large chunks)
1		red bell pepper (cut in large chunks)
4	cloves	garlic (roasted)
2	tbsp.	extra virgin olive oil
1		onion (sliced)
1/2		zucchini (thinly sliced)
2	cups	chicken broth
28	oz.	cannellini beans (washed and drained)
2	tbsp.	fresh parsley (chopped)
1	tsp.	dried rosemary
1	tbsp.	balsamic vinegar
1/2	tsp.	black pepper

Instructions

1. Preheat oven to 400°F.
2. Place peppers and unpeeled garlic on a cookie sheet and roast them in oven for 20 minutes. Set aside.
3. Heat oil in a large pot over medium heat and add the onion and zucchini. Sauté until soft.
4. Add the chicken broth and bring to a boil.
5. Add the beans, parsley and rosemary. Reduce heat and simmer for 10 minutes.
6. Slice roasted peppers thinly, peel and cut the garlic in half. Add these to the soup along with the balsamic vinegar.
7. Heat through and serve.

SIDES

3 Bean Salad

A healthy dose of fibre, protein and taste! This is great on its own for lunch or pair with Tenderloin Steaks with Mushroom Sauce.

Ingredients

2	cups	fresh green beans
1	cup	chickpeas (rinsed)
1	cup	kidney beans (rinsed)
1/4	cup	red onion (thinly sliced)
1/4	cup	red bell pepper (thinly sliced)
1		tomato (diced)
2	tbsp.	extra virgin olive oil
2	tbsp.	Dijon mustard
1 1/2	tsp.	dried basil
1/4	tsp.	black pepper
2	tbsp.	apple cider vinegar
1	tsp.	raw honey

Instructions

1. Steam green beans until tender-crisp and cool.
2. Place green beans in a large bowl with chickpeas, kidney beans, onion, pepper and tomato. Mix well.
3. In a glass jar, combine oil, mustard, vinegar, basil, honey and pepper. Shake vigorously. Pour over the salad and toss well.

A Packet of Carrots

Throw these in the oven, on the barbeque or in a fire pit...A packet of yum! These are a great accompaniment to any main dish.

Ingredients

1	lb.	carrots (peeled and cut in chunks)
1	tbsp.	fresh rosemary (chopped)
1	clove	garlic (minced)
1⁄2		orange (zested and juiced)
1	tbsp.	extra virgin olive oil

Instructions

1. Preheat oven to 400°F.
2. Fold a large sheet of aluminum foil in half and open it up again.
3. Place the carrots in the middle of one half of the foil. Sprinkle the rosemary, garlic and orange zest over the carrots. Drizzle the olive oil and juice from the orange over all of this.
4. Fold the other half of the aluminum over the carrots and seal the sides to make a foil bag.
5. Place bag on a baking tray and cook for about 45 minutes.

Beet and Spinach Salad

A simple combination with fantastic results. Serve with Chicken Florentine or Cape Halibut.

Ingredients

2	cups	baby spinach
1		apple (chopped)
1⁄4	cup	walnuts (chopped)
1		large orange (juiced)
1	tbsp.	raw honey
		black pepper (to taste)
1⁄4	cup	goat feta cheese (crumbled) (optional)
1	cup	beets (roasted and diced)

Instructions

1. Combine spinach, beets, apple and nuts in a medium salad bowl.
2. Whisk together orange juice, honey and pepper in a small bowl.
3. Toss dressing with the salad and top with feta (if using).

Celery Root Smash Up

A great and tasty alternative to mashed potatoes! Celery root is one of my favourite vegetables. It has a mild celery taste and similar density to potatoes.

Ingredients

1		sweet onion
1⁄2	tsp	Himalayan sea salt
1	tbsp.	coconut oil
1	tbsp.	extra virgin olive oil
1		Celery root

Instructions

1. Peel and cube the celery root. Put the celery cubes into a big pot with water and cook on high until tender. Drain the contents through a strainer and mash with a potato masher. Cover to keep warm and set aside.
2. Thinly slice onion, but do not mince. Place the coconut oil in a frying pan, add the onion and sprinkle with the salt. The salt will help bring out the natural juices of the onion and help with the cooking process. Cook the onion until it is browned and caramelized. If required, add a bit of water, should the pan become dry.
3. Take the mashed celery root and add the caramelized onions. Season to taste and serve warm.

Coconut Cardamom Yams

An amazing addition to a traditional feast!

Ingredients

5		yams (peeled and cut into 3/4 inch pieces)
3	tbsp.	coconut milk
2	tsp.	cardamom (ground)
1	tsp.	vanilla
		Himalayan sea salt and pepper (to taste)
1⁄8	tsp.	cayenne pepper
1⁄3	cup	pecan halves (chopped)

Instructions

1. Preheat oven to 325°F.
2. Boil yams in a large pot of boing water until soft. Drain and transfer to a large bowl or mixing stand.
3. Add coconut milk, cardamom, vanilla, sea salt, pepper and cayenne to yams. Mash until smooth. Transfer yam mixture to a 9x9 inch baking dish. Sprinkle pecans evenly over mixture.
4. Bake 45-50 minutes until edges are slightly browned.

Cranberry Quinoa

A superstar grain paired with cranberries and nuts for a delicious combo. Serve with Honey Lime Chicken Breasts or Orange Tilapia in Parchment and reserve leftovers for lunch the next day.

Ingredients

1⁄4	cup	almonds (raw)
1⁄4	cup	Brazil nuts
1 1⁄2	cups	quinoa (rinsed)
3	cups	water
1 1⁄2	cups	almond milk
1⁄2	cup	dried cranberries
1	tbsp.	lemon zest
1	tsp.	cinnamon
1⁄2	tsp.	nutmeg
1⁄4	tsp.	allspice
1⁄4	tsp.	cardamom

Instructions

1. Place almonds and Brazil nuts into a food processor and process until fine. Transfer to a small bowl and set aside.
2. Place quinoa and water into a medium sized pot and bring to a boil. Reduce heat and simmer, covered for 15 minutes.
3. Add the processed nut mixture, almond milk, cranberries, lemon zest and spices. Let mixture cook over low heat, stirring, until thickened.
4. Remove from heat and let stand, covered for a few minutes. Fluff with a fork.

Crisp Sautéed Veggies

Great with Asian inspired dishes such as the Spicy Marinated Asian Flank Steak or the Asian Salmon.

Ingredients

1	tbsp.	extra virgin olive oil
2	cloves	garlic (minced)
1	tbsp.	fresh ginger (peeled and minced)
1 1/2	cups	sugar snap peas (trimmed)
1		red bell pepper (cut in chunks)
1/2		red onion (thinly sliced)
1	cup	bean sprouts

Instructions

1. In a large skillet, heat oil over medium heat.
2. Sauté garlic and ginger in oil until fragrant.
3. Add snap peas, red pepper and onion and sauté until tender.
4. Add bean sprouts and heat through.

Curried Cauliflower

Make your own easy and delicious curry for this dish! Don't be intimidated by the lengthy ingredient list, most of the items on the list are spices that take no time to mix together.

Ingredients

3	tsp.	extra virgin olive oil
1	tbsp.	fresh ginger (peeled and finely chopped)
1		onion (chopped)
1	cup	tomatoes (chopped)
1		yellow bell pepper (sliced)
1/2	tsp.	ground cardamom
1/2	tsp.	cinnamon
1/2	tsp.	ground coriander
1	tsp.	ground cloves
1/2	tsp.	ground cumin
1/4	tsp.	turmeric
1/4	tsp.	Chili powder
1		head cauliflower (chopped coarsely)
3	cloves	garlic (minced)
1	tbsp.	lemon juice
1	tsp.	Himalayan sea salt
1/2	tsp.	black pepper
1	cup	dairy free coconut yogurt

Instructions

1. In a large skillet, heat oil and add the ginger, onion, tomato and bell pepper. Sauté over medium heat for approximately 4 minutes.
2. Combine all of the spices and add 2 tablespoons of this mixture to the onion mixture along with the cauliflower and garlic. Cook for 2 minutes.
3. Add the yogurt and bring to a boil. Reduce heat, cover and simmer for about 25 minutes or until the cauliflower is cooked through.
4. Add lemon juice, salt and pepper and serve.

Curry Lentil Pilaf

A mild curry gives this pilaf an extra kick.

Ingredients

2	tbsp.	extra virgin olive oil
1		onion (diced)
1		zucchini (diced)
1		carrot (diced)
1	clove	garlic (minced)
1	cup	brown rice
1	tbsp.	curry paste
2	cups	vegetable stock
1	can	lentils (rinsed and drained)

Instructions

1. Heat olive oil in a medium saucepan over medium heat. Add the onion, zucchini, carrot and garlic and sauté until softened.
2. Add the rice and curry paste and stir until rice is coated.
3. Pour in the vegetable stock and reduce heat to low. Cover and simmer for 20 minutes.
4. Mix lentils into rice and cook, covered, for another 5 minutes. Fluff and serve.

Deconstructed Guacamole

The same great flavour just served up a bit differently. Serve with raw veggies or as a side to Fantastic Fish Tacos.

Ingredients

2		avocados (halved)
1⁄2	cup	cherry tomatoes (halved)
1⁄2	cup	cilantro (chopped)
2		limes (cut in wedges)
1	tsp.	extra virgin olive oil

Instructions

1. Preheat grill.
2. Sprinkle olive oil over avocado and grill just until charred.
3. Mix grilled avocado, cherry tomatoes and cilantro in a dish until combined.
4. Squeeze lime wedges over mixture and serve.

Delicious Asparagus

A simple and delicious side for any main dish. Try it with Chicken Piccata.

Ingredients

1	lb.	asparagus
1	tsp.	Himalayan sea salt
2	tbsp.	extra virgin olive oil
1	tsp.	Dijon mustard
1	tbsp.	red wine vinegar

Instructions

1. Wash asparagus and snip off the ends.
2. Boil a saucepan of water and add the asparagus with the salt.
3. Cover and bring to a boil again, cooking for about 2 minutes or until asparagus is tender crisp.
4. Combine olive oil, mustard and vinegar into a bowl and whisk.
5. Drain the asparagus and drizzle the vinaigrette over spears.

Dill Salad

A dill-icious and light salad. Combine it with Chicken with Lemon and Olives and a fantastic dinner.

Ingredients

6	cups	leaf lettuce (torn into bite size pieces)
2	tbsp.	fresh dill (chopped)
1⁄2	cup	cucumber (chopped)
1⁄2	cup	fresh tomatoes (diced)
2		green onion (chopped)
2	tsp.	grainy Dijon mustard
1⁄4	cup	extra virgin olive oil
2	tsp.	raw honey
1 1⁄2	tbsp.	lemon juice

Instructions

1. Tear and wash lettuce and place in a large bowl.
2. Place chopped vegetables in bowl with lettuce.
3. Combine Dijon, olive oil, honey and lemon juice in a small container with a lid. Cover and shake vigorously.
4. Pour dressing over salad and toss to combine.

Dilled Carrots

This is the quickest and easiest side dish. Throw this together when you are short of time.

Ingredients

6		large carrots (peeled and chopped)
1	tsp.	dried dill (or 2 tbsp. fresh dill)
		Himalayan sea salt and pepper (to taste)

Instructions

1. Steam carrots until tender crisp.
2. Sprinkle carrots with dill and salt and pepper.   Stir to combine

Garlic Smashers

Mmmmm....Mashed potatoes. This dairy free version is also much lower in carbohydrates thanks to the cauliflower! Great with any main meal especially Bison Burgers or Peppered Beef with Spinach.

Ingredients

1⁄2	lb.	Yukon Gold potatoes (cut in chunks)
1	head	cauliflower (rinsed and chopped)
4	cloves	garlic (peeled and chopped)
1	tbsp.	extra virgin olive oil
2	tbsp.	almond milk
		Himalayan sea salt and pepper (to taste)

Instructions

1. Place potatoes and whole garlic cloves in a large pot of boiling water. Cook until softened.
2. In a separate pot or steamer, cook cauliflower until soft. Drain and set aside.
3. Drain potatoes and garlic and add cauliflower. Add olive oil and almond milk and mash with a potato masher. Add more milk if necessary.
4. Season with salt and pepper to taste.

Grain Less Wrap

A great gluten free replacement for flour wraps. You can make a larger batch and store in the fridge for a couple of days. These are great for lunches or quesadillas!

Ingredients

3	tbsp.	ground flaxseed
1/4	tsp.	baking powder
1	pinch	Himalayan sea salt
1	tbsp.	coconut oil (melted)
3	tbsp.	water
1		egg

Instructions

1. Mix all the dry ingredients together and set aside.
2. Mix all the wet ingredients together and pour into the dry ingredients.
3. Melt a drop of coconut oil in a frying pan, until just melted.
4. Remove pan from heat. Pour in the batter and very gently work into the shape of a thin pancake with even distribution.
5. Once done, place pan back on the stove and cook over low heat until you see the batter start to rise and get crisp along the edges.
6. Gently turn and cook until done.

Herb and Cumin Green Beans

A delicious dressing for your beans to add a fresh flavour to an old favorite!

Ingredients

1	tbsp.	extra virgin olive oil
1	tbsp.	fresh dill (finely chopped)
1	tbsp.	fresh chives (finely chopped)
1	clove	garlic (minced)
1	tsp.	lemon juice
1⁄2	tsp.	cumin
1	lb.	green beans (trimmed)
1⁄4	cup	plain dairy free coconut yogurt

Instructions

1. Combine all ingredients except green beans.
2. Boil a pot of water. Place beans in boiling water and cook for 3-4 minutes. Drain and pat dry.
3. Toss with dressing and serve.

Jeweled Brown Rice

A fantastic accompaniment to any main event! Make a double batch and freeze half for a future dinner.

Ingredients

4	tbsp.	extra virgin olive oil (divided)
1	cup	purple onion (chopped)
1/2	cup	bell pepper (chopped, any colour)
1/2	cup	carrot (chopped)
1	cup	parsnip (chopped)
1/2	cup	celery (chopped)
1/2	cup	butternut squash (chopped)
1/2	cup	zucchini (chopped)
1/2	cup	mushrooms (chopped)
1/2	cup	leeks (chopped; whites only)
1/2	cup	low sodium chicken stock
2	tsp.	gluten free tamari
		Himalayan sea salt and black pepper (to taste)
2	cups	brown rice (cooked)
1/2	cup	fresh parsley (chopped)
1/2	cup	fresh basil (chopped)

Instructions

1. Sauté all veggies in half of the olive oil in a large skillet. Set aside.
2. Heat remaining oil in large wok. Place veggies in wok and add chicken stock, tamari, salt and pepper. Stir well.
3. Stir in cooked brown rice. Heat through for about 10 minutes.
4. Before serving, add chopped herbs.

Lemon Chickpea Pilaf

A perfect accompaniment or a standalone vegetarian meal.

Ingredients

1	tbsp.	extra virgin olive oil
1		onion (diced)
1	clove	garlic (minced)
2	cups	brown rice
1/4	cup	dried cranberries
1	tbsp.	lemon rind
1/2	tsp.	cumin
1/4	tsp.	cinnamon
2	cups	chicken stock
2	cups	water
1	can	chickpeas (rinsed and drained)

Instructions

1. Heat olive oil in a medium saucepan over medium heat. Add the onion and garlic and sauté until softened.
2. Add the rice, dried cranberries, lemon rind, cumin and cinnamon and stir until rice is coated.
3. Pour in the chicken stock and water and reduce heat to low. Cover and simmer for 20 minutes.
4. Mix chickpeas into rice and cook covered for another 5 minutes. Fluff and serve.

Mediterranean Lentils

A very unique combination of Eastern spices and smooth lentils. Serve over quinoa for a complete vegetarian meal or as a side with Tomato and Basil Salmon.

Ingredients

1	cup	green lentils
2		leeks (chopped; whites only)
1	cup	fresh cilantro (chopped)
2	tsp.	fresh mint (chopped)
1	tsp.	fresh rosemary (chopped)
		fresh ground pepper (pinch)
2	tbsp.	ground coriander
2	tbsp.	red wine vinegar
3	tbsp.	fish sauce
1	tbsp.	extra virgin olive oil
1	tbsp.	raw honey

Instructions

1. Soak lentils in cold water overnight. If short on time a can of lentils can be substituted (skip step 2 and just add lentils to large saucepan).
2. Rinse and drain lentils. Place in a large saucepan and cover with water. Bring to a boil. Skim any foam off the water and reduce to simmer.
3. Add chopped leeks and fresh cilantro to lentils and stir. Add all remaining ingredients and simmer until tender, about 30 minutes.

Nutty, Herbed Green Beans

Sautéed with walnuts and tarragon, you'll ask for these again. These go great with Turkey Meatloaf or Clean Cabbage Rolls.

Ingredients

1	lb.	green beans (trimmed)
2	tbsp.	walnut oil
2	tbsp.	shallots (minced)
2	tbsp.	fresh tarragon (minced)
1/2	cup	walnuts (chopped and toasted)
		Himalayan sea salt and black pepper

Instructions

1. Boil a large pot of water and add 1/2 tsp. of salt. Add the beans and cook for 2 minutes.
2. Drain and immediately pour them into a bowl of ice water. Drain and set aside.
3. In a large skillet, heat the oil over medium heat and add the shallots. Cook for about 3 minutes or until they are soft.
4. Add the beans to the skillet and stir frequently for about 4 minutes. Stir in the tarragon and season with salt and pepper to taste.
5. Sprinkle the beans with the toasted walnuts and serve.

Orange Spinach Salad

Quickly toss this together for a light and delicious salad. Serve with Dilled Salmon Spears or Grilled Apple Chicken.

Ingredients

6	cups	spinach (washed and trimmed)
1/2	cup	mandarin oranges
1/4	cup	pecans (roughly chopped)
1/4	cup	balsamic vinaigrette

Instructions

Combine all ingredients and toss.

Roasted Green Beans

Another fantastic way to serve up green beans!

Ingredients

1	lb.	fresh green beans
2	tsp.	extra virgin olive oil
1/4	tsp.	black pepper
1/4	tsp.	dried rosemary
1/4	tsp.	dried thyme
1/4	tsp.	dried oregano
1/4	tsp.	dried marjoram
1	tbsp.	balsamic vinegar

Instructions

1. Preheat oven to 450°F. Place all of the ingredients except the vinegar in a roasting pan and stir until well mixed.
2. Bake for 10-12 minutes or until the beans are tender, stirring once.
3. Remove from the oven and drizzle balsamic vinegar over top.

Roasted Parsnips and Carrots

The mild hint of pepper from the parsnips is offset by the sweetness of the orange and carrots. This is a great side dish for any Holiday dinner.

Ingredients

2	tbsp.	extra virgin olive oil
½	cup	hot water
2	cups	parsnips (cut into 1 inch pieces)
2	cups	carrots (cut into 1 inch pieces)
1		orange (juiced)
2	tbsp.	fresh parsley (chopped)
1	tsp.	raw honey

Instructions

1. Pour the olive oil into a large skillet and heat over medium heat. Add parsnips and carrots. Cook for about 10 minutes or until they turn golden brown.
2. Combine the orange juice, 1/2 cup hot water and raw honey in a bowl and stir.
3. Pour the juice mixture into the skillet with the veggies and simmer. Reduce heat, cover and cook another 10 minutes or until the vegetables are almost tender.
4. Remove the cover, turn the heat up to medium high and cook until the liquid evaporates.
5. Sprinkle parsley over top and serve.

Roasted Veggies and Goat Cheese Macaroni

A Mediterranean twist to a classic favourite. You can omit the goat cheese if you cannot tolerate it and replace with a sprinkle of vegan Daiya mozza cheese.

Ingredients

2	cups	gluten free macaroni
1		red bell pepper (sliced into wedges)
1		green bell pepper (sliced into wedges)
1		yellow bell pepper (sliced into wedges)
1		red onion (sliced in thick semi circles)
1		zucchini (sliced into half-moons)
1		eggplant (quartered and sliced)
1	cup	cherry tomatoes (halved)
5	oz.	goat cheese (crumbled)(optional)
1	clove	garlic (minced)
2	tbsp.	extra virgin olive oil
1/2	cup	fresh chives (chopped)
1/4	cup	fresh parsley (chopped)
1/2	cup	fresh basil (chopped)
1/3	cup	red wine vinegar

Instructions

1. Cook pasta according to directions, rinse under cold water, drain and set aside.
2. Preheat oven to 400°F.
3. Place peppers and onions on a baking sheet and sprinkle with 1 tbsp. olive oil. Roast in the oven about 10 minutes or until browned. Place in a large bowl.
4. Repeat step 3 with zucchini, eggplant and tomatoes. Add to the bowl of roasted vegetables.
5. To prepare vinaigrette, blend the last 6 ingredients in a food processor to form a smooth liquid.
6. Add the pasta and vinaigrette to a large bowl with the vegetables and toss.
7. Top with goat cheese and serve.

Sautéed Collard Greens

Get your greens! Collard greens are mild tasting and do not have a bitter quality to them. They go great with Cardamom Over Roasted Chicken or Grilled Tuna and Asparagus.

Ingredients

2	tsp.	pure maple syrup
1 1⁄2	lb.	collard greens
4	cloves	garlic (minced)
1⁄2	tsp.	red pepper flakes
1	tbsp.	apple cider vinegar

Instructions

1. Whisk the vinegar and maple syrup together in a small bowl.
2. Trim the collard leaves by cutting off the stems and wash and dry. Cut the greens into half inch strips.
3. in a large nonstick skillet, heat the olive oil and garlic. Add the red pepper flakes and the collards. Stir and toss the collards until they are slightly wilted.
4. Drizzle the vinegar maple mixture over the top, stir well and serve.

Sautéed Greens

Packed full of nutrients and taste! Serve alongside Falafel Patties.

Ingredients

2	tbsp.	extra virgin olive oil
1		yellow onion (diced)
2	cloves	garlic (minced)
3	cups	spinach (chopped)
3	cups	kale (chopped)
2	cups	Swiss chard (collard greens could also be used; chopped)
1	cup	mushrooms (sliced)
2	tbsp.	gluten free tamari sauce

Instructions

1. Heat olive oil in large sauté pan. Add onion, garlic and mushrooms and sauté until soft.
2. Slowly mix in greens. Stir continuously until greens are turn bright green and are slightly wilted. Do not overcook. Remove from heat and add tamari. Toss and serve immediately.

Sautéed Greens and Beans

A perfect go-with-anything side dish or as a solo vegetarian meal.

Ingredients

2	tbsp.	extra virgin olive oil (divided)
3	cloves	garlic (thinly sliced)
1/4	tsp.	crushed red pepper
5	cups	spinach (torn into strips)
5	cups	kale (torn into strips)
1	cup	vegetable broth
1	can	cannellini beans (rinsed and drained)
1	tsp.	red wine vinegar

Instructions

1. Heat 2 tbsp. olive oil in a large skillet over medium heat. Add garlic and crushed red pepper and sauté for 1 minute.
2. Add greens by the handful and stir until beginning to wilt, then add another handful until all of the greens are in the skillet.
3. Add the broth and simmer for a few minutes.
4. Add the beans and simmer until the beans are heated through and the liquid is almost absorbed. Stir in vinegar, stir to coat and serve.

Sautéed Veggies

A quick and easy versatile side dish. Try these with the Tandoori Style Halibut or the Grilled Greek Chicken.

Ingredients

1	cup	mushrooms (sliced)
1	cup	zucchini (cubed)
1	tbsp.	extra virgin olive oil
2	cloves	garlic (minced)
1	cup	carrots (shredded)
1		red bell pepper (diced)
		Himalayan sea salt and black pepper
1⁄2	tsp.	red pepper flakes

Instructions

1. In a large nonstick skillet, heat the olive oil and sauté the garlic.
2. Add the vegetables and sauté until tender crisp
3. Season with salt, pepper and red pepper flakes and serve.

Stir Fried Veggies

Chop 'em, Fry 'em, love 'em!

Ingredients

2	tsp.	extra virgin olive oil
2	tsp.	sesame oil
½	cup	water (divided)
½	cup	onion (diced)
1	tbsp.	ginger (peeled and grated)
1	clove	garlic (minced)
2	cups	broccoli (florets)
1	cup	asparagus (cut into bite size pieces)
1	cup	mushrooms (cut into bit size pieces)
2	tbsp.	gluten free tamari
1	tbsp.	rice vinegar

Instructions

1. In a large skillet, heat the oils over medium heat. Add the onion, ginger and garlic and sauté until the onion softens.
2. Add the broccoli and a 1/4 cup water and cook for about 3 minutes. Add the asparagus and mushrooms and another 1/4 cup water. Cover and cook until the veggies are tender crisp.
3. Add the tamari and vinegar and stir constantly until the sauce begins to thicken. Season with salt and pepper to taste.

Tossed Broccoli

A great alternative to plain steamed broccoli. Serve with Stuffed Portobello Mushrooms or Mango Coconut Chicken with Black Beans.

Ingredients

4	cups	broccoli (cut into bite size pieces)
4	tbsp.	extra virgin olive oil
1 1⁄2	tbsp.	red wine vinegar
1	tsp.	Dijon mustard
1	clove	garlic (minced)
1⁄2	tsp.	dried oregano

Instructions

1. Steam broccoli until tender crisp.
2. Combine the remaining ingredients in a jar. Place lid on top and shake vigorously.
3. Toss steamed broccoli with vinaigrette.

Twisted Asparagus

Your family will love these! Great cold the next day or chopped into a salad.

Ingredients

2	cloves	garlic (minced)
1	tbsp.	extra virgin olive oil
1	tsp.	sesame oil
2	lb.	asparagus
1	tsp.	sesame seeds
1	tbsp.	raw honey
2	tsp.	gluten free tamari sauce

Instructions

1. Mix garlic, honey, tamari and oil in a small bowl.
2. Heat skillet over medium heat and pour mixture into pan.
3. Add asparagus and cook until tender crisp.
4. Sprinkle with sesame seeds and serve.

Winter Squash Puree

A delicious, colorful and nutrient rich side dish on cold winter nights. Serve with Turkey Meatloaf or Beef Biryani.

Ingredients

2	cups	butternut squash (cut into cubes)
2	cups	acorn squash (cut into cubes)
1	tbsp.	extra virgin olive oil
1⁄3	cup	chicken stock
1⁄2		orange (zested)
1 1⁄2	tsp	pure maple syrup

Instructions

1. Preheat oven to 450°F.
2. Toss mixed veggies with olive oil and a dash of sea salt. Roast in oven for approximately 40 minutes or until soft.
3. Place chicken stock and cooked veggies in a large pot with remaining ingredients and mash until combined.

Zucchini Ribbons

A tasty twist to eating your greens. Serve with Southwest Stuffed Turkey Breasts.

Ingredients

3		large zucchini
2	cloves	garlic (minced)
1	tbsp.	extra virgin olive oil
		Himalayan sea salt and pepper (to taste)
2	tsp.	lemon zest

Instructions

1. Cut zucchini lengthwise into 1/8-inch-thick slices using a vegetable peeler or spiralize.
2. In a medium skillet, heat oil over medium heat and sauté garlic. Add zucchini to skillet and sauté, stirring frequently until tender-only a few minutes. Do not overcook or it will become mushy.
3. Sprinkle with salt, pepper and lemon zest.

SEAFOOD

Asian Salmon

Done up in foil packets, these are quick and tasty!

Ingredients

16	oz.	salmon (cut into 4 fillets)
1	cup	quinoa (cooked)
2	cups	bok choy (coarsely chopped)
1⁄2	cup	shitake mushrooms (sliced)
2		green onion (chopped)
1	tbsp.	extra virgin olive oil
1	tsp.	fresh ginger (grated or chopped)
1	clove	garlic (minced)
2	tsp.	sesame oil
2	tbsp.	gluten free tamari sauce

Instructions

1. Preheat oven to 450°F.
2. Take two 12 x 24 sheets of aluminum foil and fold each sheet over to make a double thick square.
3. Brush a little oil on the center of each square.
4. Rinse the fish and prepare all of the ingredients.
5. Spread half of the quinoa on the center of each foil square and then layer the greens, shitake mushrooms, fish and scallions on top.
6. In a small bowl, combine the olive oil, grated ginger, garlic, soy sauce and sesame oil.
7. Pour half of the sauce over each serving. Fold the foil into airtight packets. Bake for 20 minutes.
8. To serve, open the foil packets (being careful of the steam) and transfer to a plate or bowl.

Asian Shrimp Salad Cups

These take no time to make and are great for a summer party. Very fresh and fun to eat!

Ingredients

1	lb.	frozen shrimp
1/2		red bell pepper (thinly sliced)
1/2		yellow bell pepper (thinly sliced)
1/2		red onion (thinly sliced)
1/2	cup	bean sprouts
1		mango (thinly sliced)
2		grapefruits (juiced)
1/4	cup	lime juice
2	tbsp.	extra virgin olive oil
1	tsp.	garlic chili sauce
1		head butter lettuce (washed and separated)

Instructions

1. Thaw shrimp and combine the next 5 ingredients in a bowl.
2. To make the dressing, combine the grapefruit juice, lime juice, oil and garlic chili sauce in a small bowl and whisk well.
3. Pour dressing over the salad and serve in the lettuce leaves.

Basil Pesto Zucchini Prawn Pasta

Pesto with your zoodles.....Mmmmmm!

Ingredients

4	cups	basil leaves
4	tbsp.	extra virgin olive oil (divided)
3	cloves	garlic (minced)
2	tbsp.	pine nuts
		Himalayan sea salt and black pepper (to taste)
1	cup	cherry tomatoes (halved)
2	tbsp.	fresh thyme
12		fresh prawns
1	cup	green beans (cut into 1/2 inch pieces)
1	tbsp.	coconut oil
2		zucchini (Spiralized or grated)

Instructions

1. In a food processor, pulse basil with 3 tbsp. olive oil to emulsify. Add the garlic and pine nuts. Season with salt and continue to process until just slightly course in texture. Set pesto aside.
2. Preheat oven to 350°F.
3. Place tomatoes in a baking dish cut side up. Sprinkle with thyme, salt and pepper and drizzle with 1 tbsp. olive oil. Bake until they begin to brown, about 15 minutes.
4. Bring 4 cups of water to a boil in a pot. Blanch beans in boiling water for 4 minutes, remove and place in cold water. Drain and set aside.
5. Melt 1 tsp. coconut oil in a small pan and sauté prawns.
6. Combine the tomatoes, pesto, beans and zucchini to prawns and sauté for an additional 2 minutes.
7. Serve.

Bean, Fish and Avocado Tacos

West Coast style tacos. Serve with a simple Side Salad or the 3 Bean Salad.

Ingredients

2		avocados (diced)
2		tomatillos (diced)
1		tomato (diced)
1		jalapeno (seeded and minced)
1	clove	garlic (minced)
1⁄4	cup	cilantro leaves (chopped)
1		lime (zested and juiced, divided)
4	tsp.	extra virgin olive oil (divided)
		Himalayan sea salt and pepper (to taste)
12	oz.	halibut (or other white fish)
1⁄2	tsp.	cumin
1⁄2	tsp.	chili powder
1⁄2	tsp.	sea salt
1	can	refried beans
8		organic non-gmo corn tortillas

Instructions

1. In a bowl combine the first 9 ingredients (half of the lime juice and half of the olive oil). Set aside for salsa.
2. Brush fish with remaining olive oil on both sides and sprinkle with the cumin, chili powder, salt and pepper. Grill for 3 minutes on each side.
3. Remove the fish from heat, cut into bite size chunks and drizzle with remaining lime juice.
4. Warm the tortillas if desired.
5. Heat the refried beans until soft.
6. Spread a spoonful of beans on each tortilla and top with pieces of fish, and a scoop of salsa.

Cape Halibut

Capers and fresh herbs add a burst of flavour to this halibut dish. This goes amazing with Sautéed Collard Greens and Celery Root Smash Up.

Ingredients

2	tbsp.	extra virgin olive oil (divided)
1/2	tsp.	black pepper (divided)
2	tbsp.	fresh parsley (chopped)
2	tbsp.	fresh basil (chopped)
2	tsp.	capers (drained and minced)
1	tsp.	shallots (minced)
1/2	tsp.	Dijon mustard
1/2		lemon (zested)
24	oz.	halibut fillets
		Himalayan sea salt (to taste)

Instructions

1. In a small bowl, mix one tbsp. olive oil, half of the pepper, parsley, basil, capers, shallots, Dijon and lemon zest. Set aside.
2. Heat the remaining 1 tbsp. olive oil in a nonstick skillet over medium heat. Sprinkle the fish with salt and pepper and add to the skillet. Cook on each side for 4 minutes or until fish flakes easily.
3. Top with caper mixture.

Citrus Fish and Quinoa

Short on time, big on flavour.

Ingredients

3	tbsp.	extra virgin olive oil
1⁄2	cup	parsley (chopped)
1		lemon (zested and juiced)
1		lime (zested and juiced)
1		orange (zested and chopped into bite size pieces)
1	tbsp.	hot pepper sauce
1	tbsp.	fresh thyme
		Himalayan sea salt and pepper (to taste)
16	oz.	halibut (in 4 pieces)
1		red bell pepper
4		green onion (chopped)
2	cups	chicken broth
1	cup	quinoa

Instructions

1. Combine 2 tbsp. olive oil, parsley, lemon juice and zest, lime juice and zest, orange zest, hot sauce and thyme in a shallow dish. Season with salt and pepper and add the halibut. Marinate for 15 minutes.
2. Preheat grill.
3. Heat the remaining 1 tbsp. olive oil in a medium saucepan over medium heat. Add the bell pepper and green onion and cook until softened.
4. Add the chicken broth and bring to a boil. Stir in the quinoa, cover and simmer for 15 minutes.
5. Grill the fish until cooked through and flakes easily.
6. Fluff the quinoa, mix in the orange pieces and serve with fish.

Curried Fish and Garden Veggies

This flavourful fish dish is low in carbs and high in taste!

Ingredients

1	tsp.	coconut oil (extra virgin olive oil can also be used)
1		onion (cut into crescent moons)
4		carrots (sliced diagonally)
4	cloves	garlic (crushed)
1	tsp.	turmeric
1	can	coconut milk
1	cup	low sodium chicken broth
4	tsp.	red curry paste
2	tbsp.	fish sauce
2		red bell peppers (cut into 1 inch pieces)
2		tomatoes (diced small)
2	lb.	fresh halibut (skin removed; cut into 1 inch cubes (other white fish can be substituted)
1	cup	fresh basil leaves (thinly sliced)
2		zucchini (cut into half-moons)

Instructions

1. In an 11-inch skillet or other large pan, heat the oil over medium-high heat. Add the onions and sauté for about 5 minutes. Add the carrots and garlic and sauté a few minutes more.
2. Add the turmeric, coconut milk, chicken broth, red curry paste and fish sauce. Stir to incorporate the curry paste. Simmer for about 5 to 7 minutes or until carrots are almost cooked.
3. Add the zucchini and bell peppers. Simmer until the veggies are crisp-tender then add the tomatoes and fish and simmer until fish flakes easily. Be careful not to stir too much otherwise the fish will fall apart. Sprinkle with basil and serve hot!

Dilled Salmon Skewers

A fresh and simple way to create a tasty salmon dish. Serve with Roasted Beets and Orange Slices or the Dill Salad.

Ingredients

24	oz.	salmon fillet
3	tbsp.	fresh dill (chopped)
2	tbsp.	extra virgin olive oil
1		lemon (zested and juiced)
8		lemon wedges
1/2	tsp.	Himalayan sea salt
1/4	tsp	black pepper
		hot pepper sauce (to taste)

Instructions

1. Remove the skin from the salmon and cut into 1 1/2 inch cubes.
2. Mix together the dill, oil, 1 tsp lemon rind, 2 tbsp. lemon juice, salt, pepper and hot sauce in a large bowl.
3. Add the salmon cubes to the above mixture, toss to coat and let it stand for 20 minutes.
4. Place a lemon wedge on a metal skewer, thread about 4 salmon pieces on the skewer and add another lemon wedge to the end. Repeat to make 4 skewers.
5. Place on a preheated grill and brush each skewer with the marinade.
6. Grill until fish flakes easily, about 10 minutes.

Easy Peasy Shrimp Stir Fry

Black bean noodles can be found in most grocery stores. Make sure to rinse them thoroughly after cooking.

Ingredients

2	inch	piece of fresh ginger (chopped)
2	cloves	garlic (chopped)
1/2	cup	fresh cilantro (chopped)
1	tbsp.	extra virgin olive oil
1	lb.	shrimp (peeled)
1	tsp.	5 spice powder
1	tsp.	arrowroot powder
1⁄2	cup	organic baby corn
1	cup	snow peas
2	tbsp.	gluten free tamari
1		lime (juiced)
1⁄2	tsp.	red pepper flakes
1	tsp.	raw honey
1	tsp.	sesame oil
1⁄2	cup	frozen peas
1⁄2	cup	bean sprouts
1	cup	buckwheat soba noodles or black bean noodles (cooked)

Instructions

1. In a large skillet or wok, heat the olive oil over high heat and add the ginger, garlic, red pepper flakes, shrimp and 5 spice powder and fry for 1 minute.
2. Add the arrowroot powder, baby corn and snow peas to the wok and stir for another minute.
3. Stir in the tamari, lime juice, honey, sesame oil and peas.
4. Divide soba or black bean noodles among plates and spoon the shrimp and veggies over top.
5. Sprinkle with bean sprouts and cilantro leaves.

Fantastic Fish Tacos

These are simply delicious!

Ingredients

3		6 oz. filets of Mahi Mahi (or other firm white fish)
3	tbsp.	extra virgin olive oil (divided)
1		jalapeno Chile (seeded and minced)
1		red onion (finely chopped)
1	clove	garlic (minced)
1	can	black beans (rinsed)
		Himalayan sea salt and black pepper
1	tsp.	cumin
2	tbsp.	raw honey
1	tbsp.	hot pepper sauce
2		limes (zested and juiced)
1/2		red cabbage (shredded)
1/2	cup	cilantro (finely chopped)
8		organic non-gmo corn tortillas

Instructions

1. Heat 1 tbsp. olive oil in a medium skillet over medium heat. Add the jalapeno, a quarter of the red onion and garlic. Cook for 4 minutes.
2. Mash the beans in a small bowl and add the cumin as well as a dash of salt and pepper.
3. Combine 1 tbsp. oil with honey, hot sauce and lime juice. Add the remaining red onion, cabbage and cilantro, toss and set aside.
4. Preheat a grill and coat the fish with remaining tbsp. of olive oil and lime zest. Grill fish for 8 minutes, turning once.
5. Warm the tortillas and spread a few spoonfuls of the mashed beans on the tortillas.
6. Flake half a piece of fish onto each tortilla and top with some cabbage slaw.

Ginger Miso Salmon

A quick, tasty and nutritious meal you'll love. Serve with Delicious Asparagus and Garlic Mashers for a larger meal.

Ingredients

1	tbsp.	miso paste
1	tbsp.	sesame oil
1⁄2	tbsp.	rice vinegar
1	tbsp.	fresh ginger (minced)
1	clove	garlic (minced)
1⁄2	tsp.	onion powder
1	tbsp.	sesame seeds
1	tbsp.	coconut oil
4		wild salmon steaks (6-8 oz. each)
10	cups	spinach (it shrinks!)

Instructions

1. Mix the first 7 ingredients together with 2 tablespoons water until the miso paste dissolves. Set aside.
2. In a large skillet, heat the coconut oil over medium heat. Cook the salmon steaks for about 5 minutes.
3. Turn the steaks over and place the spinach on top.
4. Pour the miso paste mixture over the spinach.
5. Place a lid over the skillet and cook for 3-4 minutes or until the salmon is clear and easily flakes and the spinach is wilted.
6. Place the salmon on plates with the spinach over top and drizzle any of the extra pan juices.

Greek Fish Fillets

Tilapia with a Greek flair. This combines well with Mediterranean Lentils.

Ingredients

4		tilapia fillets
1/4	tsp	Himalayan sea salt and pepper
1	tbsp.	extra virgin olive oil
1	tbsp.	lime juice
1		small red onion (finely chopped)
1/2	cup	Greek olives
1	tsp.	dried dill
1/2	tsp.	paprika
1	clove	garlic (minced)

Instructions

1. Sprinkle tilapia with salt and pepper and place on a broiler pan.
2. Combine olive oil and lime juice in a small bowl and vigorously stir. Add in the onion, olives and seasonings.
3. Spread mixture over tilapia fillets.
4. Broil for 6-9 minutes or until fish flakes easily.

Grilled Tuna and Asparagus

You'll be surprised at how easy this is to prepare. The sun dried tomatoes and red Chile really give this dish a kick.

Ingredients

1	bunch	asparagus (trimmed)
2	tbsp.	extra virgin olive oil (divided)
4		tuna steaks (1/2 inch thick)
1/2	cup	fresh basil (chopped)
1/2		red Chile (seeded and chopped)
1/4	cup	sun dried tomatoes (chopped)
1/2		lemon (juiced)
1	tbsp.	balsamic vinegar

Instructions

1. In a bowl, combine the basil, Chile, sun dried tomatoes, lemon juice, 1 tbsp. olive oil and balsamic vinegar. Set aside.
2. Put a large grill pan on high heat and let it get really hot.
3. Drizzle the remaining olive oil over the tuna and season with salt and pepper to taste.
4. Place the asparagus in the hot pan, turning them frequently so they don't burn. After a few minutes, push them to one side of the pan and add the tuna.
5. When the tuna has cooked halfway through (a minute or so), flip steaks over and cook for another minute or so. The tuna should remain a little pink in the middle when you serve it.
6. To serve, place a few asparagus spears on each plate, add a spoonful of tangy mixture on top, place tuna on top of this and add another spoonful of mixture.

Halibut with Carrots and Leeks

Easy and delicious! This dish is so simple; it can be thrown together in a matter of minutes.

Ingredients

4		carrots (thinly sliced)
2		leeks (sliced)
4		halibut fillets (1-inch-thick; skin removed) (or other white fish)
4	tbsp.	extra virgin olive oil
1⁄2	cup	fresh oregano (chopped)
		Himalayan sea salt and black pepper (to taste)

Instructions

1. Preheat oven to 375°F.
2. Make 4 parchment squares
3. Place the carrots and leeks in the center of each square. Place the halibut on top of the vegetables.
4. Season with salt and pepper. Drizzle with the olive oil, and sprinkle with oregano.
5. Fold the parchment over several times to seal. Place a single layer on a baking sheet. Bake for 25 minutes. Remove from the oven, and transfer each packet to a plate.

Halibut with Tomatoes and Herbs

Fresh herbs add a punch of flavour to this dish. This can be served on its own or over quinoa or brown rice.

Ingredients

1 1/2	lb.	halibut (or other white fish)
4	tbsp.	fresh lemon juice
1/2	tsp.	Himalayan sea salt
1	tbsp.	extra virgin olive oil
1	tsp.	Italian seasoning
2	cloves	garlic (minced)
2		zucchini (chopped)
1/2	cup	Kalamata olives
14	oz.	can diced tomatoes
1/2	cup	fresh basil
2	tsp.	fresh oregano (chopped)

Instructions

1. Cut the skin from the halibut and place on a plate. Cover with lemon juice and sea salt. Let sit for 10 minutes.
2. Heat olive oil in a large skillet over medium heat. Add onion and sauté until it turns golden.
3. Add Italian seasoning, garlic, zucchini and olives. Sauté 5 more minutes.
4. Move the vegetables to the side of the pan and add the halibut. Cook for 3 minutes and flip.
5. Add the tomatoes, basil, oregano and a little water if needed.
6. Cover and simmer on low until the halibut flakes easily, about 10 minutes.

Hurried Curried Tuna Salad

For those "I need dinner fast" kind of evenings. This is also great as leftovers for lunch the next day.

Ingredients

2	can	light tuna in water (drained)
2	tbsp.	plain coconut yoghurt or organic mayonnaise
1	tsp.	curry powder
1		tomato (chopped)
1		green bell pepper (chopped)
1		red bell pepper (chopped)
1	cup	cucumber (peeled and chopped)
2		celery stalks (chopped)
1⁄4	cup	onion (chopped)
2	tbsp.	balsamic vinaigrette

Instructions

1. In a small bowl, combine the tuna, yogurt or organic mayonnaise and curry powder with a fork. Set aside.
2. In a medium sized bowl, combine the tomatoes, pepper, cucumber, celery and onion.
3. Toss the vegetables with the vinaigrette dressing.
4. Evenly distribute the vegetable mixture amongst 4 plates and place a scoop of the tuna on top of the vegetables.

Orange Tilapia in Parchment

The citrus in this recipe really makes this dish come to life. Serve this with the Green Quinoa Salad.

Ingredients

1⁄4	cup	orange juice
2		oranges (zested)
1⁄4	tsp.	Himalayan sea salt
1⁄4	tsp.	cayenne pepper
1⁄4	tsp.	black pepper
4		tilapia fillets
1	cup	carrot (julienned)
1	cup	zucchini (julienned)
4	pieces	parchment paper

Instructions

1. Combine the first 5 ingredients in a small bowl and set aside.
2. Cut 4 pieces of parchment paper into 18 x 12 inch lengths. Place a piece of fish on top of each piece of paper. Divide the carrots and zucchini evenly and place on top of each filet of fish. Drizzle with orange juice mixture.
3. Fold the parchment paper over the fish and crimp the sides to seal. Repeat the process for all four fillets and place on a baking sheet.
4. Bake at 450°F for about 15 minutes or until the fish flakes easily with a fork.

Roasted Halibut with Orange Salsa

Another citrus twist with white fish. The orange salsa really makes this dish. Serve with Lemon Chickpea Pilaf or the Orange Spinach Salad.

Ingredients

2		navel oranges (zested and juiced)
2		blood oranges (cut into bite size pieces)
2	tbsp.	red onion (minced)
1	tbsp.	cilantro (chopped)
3	tbsp.	extra virgin olive oil (divided)
1	tsp.	fresh thyme (chopped)
24	oz.	halibut (in four fillets) (or other white fish)

Instructions

1. Preheat the oven to 425°F.
2. Boil the orange juice in a saucepan for about 8 minutes or until reduced to 1/4 cup. Let cool.
3. Mix the reduced orange juice, orange segments, onion, cilantro, olive oil and 1 tbsp. orange zest in a medium bowl and season with salt and pepper.
4. Mix the remaining orange zest, thyme and a dash of salt and pepper in a small bowl. Rub all over the halibut fillets.
5. Heat 2 tbsp. olive oil in a nonstick skillet over medium heat and add the fillets. Sear the halibut for about for about 2 minutes or until browned on one side. Flip the pieces and place the skillet in the oven.
6. Roast the halibut until it is cooked through, about another 4-5 minutes. Remove from the pan and place on the plates. Serve with the orange salsa.

Salmon and Spinach Salad with Mustard Vinaigrette

A delicious and hearty salad packed with protein. The sautéed onions and vinaigrette allow the spinach to slightly soften and make this a warm salad for any season.

Ingredients

24	oz.	salmon fillet
1/2	tsp	black pepper
1/2	tsp	Himalayan sea salt
3	tbsp.	extra virgin olive oil
1/2		red onion (thinly sliced)
1	tsp.	dried dill
2	tbsp.	grainy mustard
2	tbsp.	red wine vinegar
6	cups	fresh spinach
1/4	cup	almond slivers
1		lemon (juiced)

Instructions

1. Preheat grill.
2. Season salmon fillet with salt, pepper and dill. Sprinkle lemon juice over top. Place on grill and cook until the salmon flakes easily.
3. In a medium skillet, heat the olive oil over medium heat. Add the onion and sauté until softened. Whisk in the mustard and vinegar.
4. Distribute the spinach evenly among 4 plates, sprinkle the almonds over top and pour the onions and vinaigrette over top of the spinach.
5. Divide the salmon into 4 portions and place each portion on top of the divided spinach.

Salmon Salad with Chickpeas and Tomatoes

The classic combination of Salmon and Capers nestled within a symphony of citrus and Mediterranean flavours.

Ingredients

2	tbsp.	extra virgin olive oil
24	oz.	salmon fillet
1 1⁄2	cups	chickpeas (rinsed and drained)
1	cup	tomatoes (chopped)
		Himalayan sea salt and black pepper (to taste)
1⁄4	cup	black olives
2	tbsp.	flat leaf parsley (chopped)
1		orange (zested and juiced)
1		lemon (zested and juiced)
2	tbsp.	capers (rinsed and drained)
2	tbsp.	fresh basil (roughly chopped)
6	cups	salad greens

Instructions

1. Preheat grill. Season salmon with salt and pepper. Place on grill and cook until the salmon flakes easily. Cool and break into small pieces.
2. In a large skillet, heat the olive oil over medium heat. Add the chickpeas and the rest of the ingredients (except the basil and salad greens) to the skillet. Stir and cook until heated through. Season with sea salt and pepper if desired.
3. Divide salad greens among your plates, place a large scoop of the chickpea mixture over the greens and scatter the salmon over the chickpeas.
4. Sprinkle the basil over the salad and serve.

Sautéed Asparagus and Shrimp

Shrimp and asparagus go so well together especially with a hint of red pepper flakes. Serve this with Nutty, Herbed Beans and A Packet of Carrots.

Ingredients

1⁄4	cup	parsley (chopped)
1		lemon (zested)
		Himalayan sea salt and black pepper (to taste)
3	cloves	garlic (minced)
2	tbsp.	extra virgin olive oil (divided)
3	cups	asparagus (trimmed)
1 1⁄2	lb.	shrimp (peeled and deveined)
1⁄2	tsp.	red pepper flakes

Instructions

1. Combine the first 4 ingredients and set aside.
2. Heat 1 tbsp. olive oil in a large nonstick skillet over medium heat. Add the asparagus and sauté for 3 minutes, stirring often. Remove the asparagus from the pan and keep warm.
3. Add the remaining olive oil to the skillet and heat. Add the shrimp and sauté for about 3 minutes or until no longer pink.
4. Add the asparagus, salt and pepper and red pepper flakes.
5. Sprinkle with the reserved parsley mixture.

Shrimp and Pineapple Fried Rice

Throw this together with ease for a new found favorite. For a lower carb version substitute cauliflower rice instead.

Cauliflower Rice:
Grate 1/2 head of cauliflower into rice like pieces.

Add to a skillet with 1 tsp coconut or extra virgin olive oil and sauté for 5 minutes. Season with sea salt and ground black pepper.

Ingredients

2		eggs (whisked)
1		onion (chopped)
1	tsp.	extra virgin olive oil
3	cloves	garlic (minced)
3	cups	cooked brown rice or Cauliflower Rice
1	can	unsweetened pineapple chunks (drained)
1/2	lb.	shrimp (peeled and deveined)
1/2	cup	cashews (chopped)
1/2	cup	frozen peas
2		green onions (sliced)
3	tbsp.	tamari sauce
1	tsp.	sesame oil
1/2	tsp.	red pepper flakes

Instructions

1. Heat olive oil in a large nonstick skillet over medium heat. Add the eggs and cook until set. Remove and keep warm.
2. In the same skillet, sauté the onion in the remaining oil until soft.
3. Add the garlic and cook for another minute. Stir in the rice, pineapple, shrimp, cashews, peas and green onion. Heat through.
4. Combine the tamari, sesame oil and red pepper flakes. Stir into the rice mixture. Stir in eggs.

Shrimp and Quinoa Veggie Scramble

A delicious mix of roasted veggies, seafood and grains. This is also fantastic as a cold salad for lunchtime leftovers.

Ingredients

2	tbsp.	extra virgin olive oil
1		onion (cut into wedges)
1	cup	mushrooms (halved)
1		green bell pepper (cut into 1 inch pieces)
1		red bell pepper (cut into 1 inch pieces)
2		zucchini (1/2 inch slices)
2	tsp.	Italian seasoning
1⁄2	cup	chicken stock
2	cups	spinach (chopped)
2	cloves	garlic (minced)
12	oz.	shrimp (tailed and deveined)
1⁄2	cup	parsley
1⁄4	cup	pine nuts
1	cup	quinoa
2	cups	water

Instructions

1. Boil 2 cups of water, add the quinoa. Reduce heat, cover and simmer for 15 minutes.
2. Preheat oven to 425°F.
3. Place the olive oil, onion, mushrooms, peppers and zucchini in a large bowl. Season with salt and pepper and toss to coat. Place in the oven and roast for about 50 minutes. Set aside.
4. Place the cooked quinoa in a saucepan along with the Italian seasoning, chicken stock, spinach, garlic and 1 tbsp. olive oil. Cook until the spinach begins to wilt.
5. Add the shrimp and parsley and cook until the shrimp turns pink.
6. Fold in the roasted veggies and sprinkle the pine nuts on top.

Shrimp with Spaghetti Squash and Spinach

This is so easy to make that it is bound to become a regular meal!

Ingredients

1		spaghetti squash (halved and seeds scooped out)
1	lb.	shrimp (peeled and deveined)
4	cloves	garlic (minced)
2	tsp.	extra virgin olive oil
1⁄3	cup	chicken broth
1⁄2	tsp.	Himalayan sea salt (divided)
	pinch	red pepper flakes
4	cups	spinach
2	tbsp.	pine nuts (toasted)

Instructions

1. Preheat oven to 350°F.
2. Place squash, flesh down, on a baking sheet and bake until easily pierced with a fork, 40-50 minutes.
3. Place 1 teaspoon olive oil in a medium skillet and sauté 2 cloves garlic.
4. Add shrimp and sauté until pink. Remove from skillet and set aside.
5. Add remaining olive oil to skillet and sauté the remaining 2 cloves of garlic.
6. Stir in broth, salt and red pepper flakes. Add spinach, handfuls at a time and cook until wilted.
7. When squash is done, use a fork to separate strands and distribute onto plates evenly.
8. Divide cooked spinach and place on top of squash, place shrimp on top of spinach, and sprinkle pine nuts over top.

Smoky Shrimp and Chorizo Pan Roast

Shrimp, turkey sausage and veggies all jumbled together for a Spanish infused meal.

Ingredients

1	lb.	small red new potatoes (halved)
2	tbsp.	extra virgin olive oil
3/4	tsp	Himalayan sea salt (divided)
1/2	tsp	black pepper (divided)
1	lb.	large shrimp (deveined)
1	lb.	green beans (trimmed and cut into 1 1/2" pieces)
4	cloves	garlic (chopped)
1/2	cup	vegetable broth
1/2	tsp.	smoked paprika
2		red bell peppers (cut into thin strips)
1/4	cup	parsley (chopped)
1/4	lb.	spicy turkey sausage (thinly sliced)

Instructions

1. Preheat oven to 400°F.
2. In a large roasting pan combine potatoes, olive oil, 1/2 teaspoon sea salt, and 1/4 teaspoon pepper. Toss to coat.
3. Arrange potatoes in a layer, cut side down, in pan. Bake for 15 minutes or until browned.
4. While potatoes cook, peel shrimp and set aside.
5. Remove potatoes from oven. Add the sausage, beans, garlic and remaining salt and pepper into the pan. Bake for 10 minutes. Add the vegetable stock, paprika, bell pepper and shrimp and bake for another 10 minutes or until veggies are tender and shrimp is done.
6. Sprinkle with parsley and serve.

Tandoori Style Halibut

Curry and a yogurt marinade give this a delicious Indian flair. Serve with Curried Quinoa.

Ingredients

2	tsp.	extra virgin olive oil
2	tbsp.	lemon juice
1	tbsp.	cilantro (chopped)
1	tbsp.	fresh dill (chopped)
1⁄2	tsp.	Himalayan sea salt
1⁄2	tsp.	curry powder
1⁄2	tsp.	sweet paprika
1 1⁄2	lb.	halibut (cut into 4 pieces)
1	cup	plain dairy free coconut milk yogurt

Instructions

1. Combine the yogurt, lemon juice, cilantro, dill, salt, curry and paprika in a bowl and whisk.
2. Dip each piece of fish in the yogurt mixture and coat on both sides. Place the fish on a lined baking sheet and pour any extra marinade over top.
3. Let fish marinate in the fridge for at least 20 minutes. Preheat oven to 375°F.
4. Bake the halibut for about 15 minutes or until cooked through.

Thai Coconut Shrimp

Sure to be a family favorite! Serve on its own or over quinoa or brown rice.

Ingredients

2	cups	broccoli (cut into bite sized florets)
2⁄3	cup	coconut milk
1	tbsp.	tomato paste
3	tbsp.	natural peanut butter
1	tsp.	ginger
4	cloves	garlic (minced)
1⁄2	tsp.	red pepper flakes
1		lime (juiced)
1		red bell pepper (sliced)
1	cup	bean sprouts
24		medium shrimp (peeled and deveined)

Instructions

1. Boil a pot of water and add broccoli. Reduce heat and simmer for 4-6 minutes. Drain and set aside.
2. Add coconut milk, tomato paste, peanut butter, ginger, garlic, pepper flakes and lime juice in a bowl and whisk to combine.
3. Over medium heat, simmer coconut milk mixture, bell peppers and bean sprouts for 5 minutes.
4. Add shrimp and cook until shrimp turn pink.
5. Toss broccoli with coconut shrimp mixture and serve.

Thai Roasted Red Pepper and Seafood Soup

Thai inspired goodness to warm your insides...

Ingredients

2		red bell peppers (seeded and quartered)
4		roma tomatoes (cored and cut in half)
1		onion (cut in wedges)
2	tbsp.	extra virgin olive oil
1/2	tsp.	Himalayan sea salt
1/2	tsp.	cumin
1/2	tsp.	coriander
3	cloves	garlic (minced)
1	tbsp.	fresh ginger (peeled and minced)
1	tbsp.	red curry paste
4	cups	chicken stock
1	can	coconut milk
1	tbsp.	fish sauce
3/4	cup	baby shrimp (or cooked crabmeat if desired)
3	tbsp.	fresh cilantro (chopped)

Instructions

1. Preheat oven to 450°F. Place peppers, tomatoes and onion on a baking sheet. Mix olive 1 1/2 tbsp. oil and spices together and toss with vegetables.
2. Roast vegetables for about 45 minutes or until tender. Let cool and remove skins from tomatoes and peppers if desired.
3. Heat remaining 1/2 tbsp. olive oil in a large pot over medium heat. Toss in garlic and ginger and sauté. Add curry paste and sauté another 30 seconds or until fragrant.
4. Add roasted vegetables and stir. Add chicken stock and simmer for about 10 minutes.
5. Using a food processor or hand blender, process mixture until smooth.
6. Stir in coconut milk and simmer, being careful not to let it boil. Add the fish sauce, shrimp and cilantro, heat through and serve.

Tilapia Florentine

Simple ingredients, fantastic taste. This is one of the easiest recipes for a last minute meal.

Ingredients

4		tilapia fillets
1⁄2	cup	grape tomatoes (halved)
2	cloves	garlic (sliced)
2	tbsp.	parsley (chopped)
1⁄2		lemon (juiced)
3		shallots (diced)
1	tbsp.	extra virgin olive oil
3	cups	spinach

Instructions

1. Preheat oven to 350°F.
2. Place fish and tomatoes in an oven proof dish and sprinkle with garlic and parsley. Drizzle lemon juice over the top.
3. Cover and bake for 15 minutes or until fish is opaque and flakes easily.
4. Over medium heat, sauté shallots in oil. Reduce heat and add spinach. Cook until wilted. Season with salt and pepper.
5. Distribute spinach evenly among 4 plates and lay one fillet over top with tomatoes.

Tomato and Basil Salmon

This is a delicious way to serve salmon. Combine this with Roasted Parsnips and Carrots.

Ingredients

2	lb.	wild salmon filet
1		lemon (juiced)
1/4	cup	extra virgin olive oil
1/4	cup	balsamic vinegar
1	cup	fresh basil leaves
3	cloves	garlic (peeled)
2	tsp.	lemon zest
1	cup	plum tomatoes (chopped)
1/2	cup	Kalamata olives
1	tbsp.	olive oil
1/4	cup	gluten free tamari

Instructions

1. Place salmon skin side up in a baking dish. Place next six ingredients in a food processor and pulse to make marinade. Pour over salmon and refrigerate for at least 1 hour.
2. Preheat oven to 400. Drain marinade (reserve about 3 tbsp.) from the salmon and place salmon skin side down in baking dish and pour reserved marinade over top. Bake salmon for 10 minutes per inch of thickness.
3. While salmon is baking, place the remaining ingredients in a bowl and mix to combine.
4. When serving salmon, spoon tomato topping over the salmon.

MAIN DISHES

Artichoke Lemon Chicken

Fresh and tangy, a delicious way to serve chicken. Life is better with artichokes!

Ingredients

1⁄2	tbsp.	dried oregano
		salt and pepper (to taste)
1	lb.	chicken cutlets
2	tbsp.	extra virgin olive oil
1		onion (thinly sliced)
2	cloves	garlic (minced)
1⁄4	can	chicken stock
1	can	artichoke hearts (drained and chopped)
2		lemons (juiced)
1	tsp.	lemon zest
2	tbsp.	parsley (chopped)
1⁄4	cup	rice flour (or other gluten free flour)

Instructions

1. In a shallow dish, combine flour and spices. Dredge cutlets in flour and set aside.
2. Heat 1 tbsp. olive oil in a large nonstick skillet over medium heat. Add chicken and cook until lightly browned on all sides and cooked through. Place on a plate and set aside, keeping warm.
3. Over medium low heat, sauté the onion in the remaining oil until soft.
4. Add garlic, sauté for 1 minute, add chicken stock and simmer. Add the artichokes, lemon juice and zest, cook for another few minutes until heated through. Season with salt and pepper.
5. Pour artichoke mixture over chicken and sprinkle with parsley.

Cardamom Oven Roasted Chicken

Throw this simple marinade together for a delicious, no hassle meal.

Preparing the marinade and chicken the night before will take minutes and save you a bundle of time at dinner time!

Ingredients

4	cloves	garlic (minced)
3	tbsp.	gluten free tamari
2	tbsp.	rice vinegar
2	tsp.	raw honey
1/4	tsp.	ground cardamom
4		boneless, skinless chicken breasts
3/4	tsp.	Himalayan sea salt
2/3	tsp.	fresh ground pepper

Instructions

1. Place the garlic, tamari, vinegar, honey, cardamom and chicken in a Ziploc bag and shake to coat the chicken. Marinate for up to 24 hours.
2. Preheat oven to 400°F.
3. Remove the chicken from the marinade, place on a baking sheet and season with the salt and pepper.
4. Bake in the oven for 35 minutes or until cooked through.

Caribbean Marinated Chicken

Spice it up, spice it down, whatever you please!

Ingredients

3	can	coconut milk
2		oranges (squeezed for juice)
3	clove	garlic cloves (minced)
1	tbsp.	fresh ginger (chopped)
1		lime (zested)
1	tsp.	allspice
1		hot pepper (minced - optional)
4		boneless, skinless, chicken breasts
1	tsp.	extra virgin olive oil
		salt and pepper (to taste)
2	cups	pineapple (diced small)

Instructions

1. In a medium bowl, whisk together first 7 ingredients to create marinade.
2. Place chicken in marinade (reserving 1/4 cup for later) and let sit up to 12 hours in refrigerator.
3. Preheat oven to 400°F.
4. In a large skillet over medium heat, add oil and brown chicken. Sprinkle with salt and pepper to taste. Remove from skillet and place in an oven proof dish in the oven until chicken is no longer pink, 10-12 minutes.
5. Mix pineapple with reserved marinade and serve over chicken.

Chicken and Bean Casserole

This can also be made in a slow cooker to save on time!

Ingredients

2 1/2	cups	dried white beans
1	tbsp.	extra virgin olive oil
6		chicken thighs
1		onion (diced)
3		carrots (peeled and diced)
3		celery stalks (diced)
2	tbsp.	fresh ginger (minced)
4	clove	garlic (minced)
14	oz.	diced tomatoes
1/4	can	tomato paste
4	cups	chicken stock
1/2	cup	cilantro (chopped)
		Himalayan salt and pepper (to taste)

Instructions

1. Soak beans in water overnight.
2. Preheat oven to 300°F.
3. Heat oil in a large pot over medium heat. Brown chicken and set aside.
4. In the same pot, sauté the onion, carrots, celery and ginger for about 8 minutes or until softened.
5. Drain the beans and add to the pot along with the garlic, tomatoes, tomato paste and chicken stock. Stir and bring to a boil.
6. Remove from heat and press the chicken into the beans. Cover and bake until the beans are tender, about 2 hours.
7. Remove from the oven and divide chicken up among plates. Add the cilantro to the bean mixture and stir.
8. Add salt and pepper to the beans and serve with the chicken.

Chicken and Black Bean Bake

A little Mexican flair for the family to enjoy!

Ingredients

4		boneless, skinless chicken breasts
1	tsp.	Cajun seasoning
1	can	black beans (drained and rinsed)
1	can	corn (drained)
1 1⁄2	cups	fresh salsa (divided)
1	can	chopped green Chile peppers (optional)
1⁄4	cup	cilantro (chopped and divided)
1	cup	Vegan Daiya cheddar cheese (optional)

Instructions

1. Heat oven to 350°F.
2. Sprinkle the chicken all over with Cajun seasoning.
3. Combine the drained beans, corn, 1 cup of the salsa, green Chile peppers and half of the cilantro.
4. Put the mixture into a casserole style baking dish.
5. Arrange chicken over the bean and corn mixture, then spoon the remaining salsa over the chicken.
6. Sprinkle with the remaining cilantro and top evenly with the cheese.
7. Cover tightly with foil and bake for 30 minutes.
8. Remove the foil and continue baking for 10 minutes, or until chicken is tender and juices run clear.

Chicken and Wild Rice Salad

A hearty one dish delight! A store bought rotisserie chicken or left over chicken is great for this dish and saves on time.

Ingredients

1	cup	wild rice (rinsed)
1	tsp.	salt
2	cups	cooked chicken
1/2	cup	celery (chopped)
1/2	cup	pecans (chopped)
2		oranges
1/4	cup	Balsamic vinaigrette dressing
1/4	cup	celery leaves

Instructions

1. In a medium pot, place the salt and rice in 3 cups of water, cover and bring to a boil.
2. Reduce heat and cook slowly until the rice is tender, about 45 minutes.
3. Place the rice, chicken, celery and nuts in a large bowl and combine.
4. Peel the oranges and cut into small segments.
5. Toss the salad with the vinaigrette, celery leaves and serve.

Chicken Breast with Sun Dried Tomatoes and Olives

Straight out of Tuscany...

Ingredients

4		boneless, skinless chicken breasts
		Himalayan salt and pepper (to taste)
1/2	cup	green olives (sliced)
1/2	cup	sun dried tomatoes (thinly sliced)
1/4	cup	gluten free flour (any variety or blend)
1/2		lemon (juiced)
1/4	cup	chicken stock

Instructions

1. Season chicken with salt and pepper. Dredge with flour.
2. Heat the oil in a large skillet and cook chicken breasts on medium heat. Brown on both sides.
3. Add the sun dried tomatoes and olives and cook for another couple of minutes. Add lemon juice and chicken stock, cook for another minute and serve.

Chicken Cacciatore

A classic chicken dish that is loved by all.

Ingredients

1	tbsp.	extra virgin olive oil
3		chicken breasts (cut into 1 inch pieces)
1		onion (finely chopped)
1⁄2		red bell pepper (chopped)
3	cloves	garlic (chopped)
1		zucchini (cut into cubes)
1⁄2		leek (chopped)
1	cup	mushrooms (sliced)
1	can	stewed tomatoes
1	cup	tomato sauce
1 1⁄2	tsp.	rosemary
1⁄2	tsp.	sea salt
1⁄4	tsp.	pepper
2	cups	wild rice (cooked)

Instructions

1. Heat olive oil in a large cooking pot and add chicken. Sauté for about 8 minutes or until browned. Remove from pot and set aside.
2. Place the onion, bell pepper, garlic, zucchini, leeks and mushrooms to the pot and sauté until soft.
3. Add tomatoes with juice, tomato sauce, chicken and rosemary. Simmer, covered for 10 minutes. Add salt and pepper and serve over rice.

Chicken Dionaea

A tasty and simple meal that the whole family will enjoy.

Ingredients

2	tbsp.	extra virgin olive oil
2	tbsp.	Dijon mustard
1	tbsp.	fresh rosemary (chopped)
1	tbsp.	fresh thyme (chopped)
2	cloves	garlic (minced)
1⁄4	tsp.	sea salt
4		boneless, skinless chicken breasts

Instructions

1. Combine the olive oil, mustard, rosemary, thyme, garlic, salt and a dash of pepper in a small bowl and mix thoroughly.
2. Preheat the oven to 400°F.
3. Place the chicken in a plastic bag along with the mustard marinade and seal. Shake until the chicken is evenly coated and refrigerate for at least 20 minutes.
4. Place in a baking dish and bake in the oven for about 20 minutes or until cooked through and no longer pink inside.

Chicken Florentine

A dish any to make any Italian Mama proud!

Ingredients

1	tsp.	extra virgin olive oil
4		boneless, skinless chicken breasts
14	oz.	crushed tomatoes
2	cloves	garlic (minced)
1	tsp.	basil
1	tsp.	dried oregano
2	cups	fresh spinach
		Himalayan salt and pepper (to taste)

Instructions

1. Heat oil in a large skillet and cook chicken until browned on each side.
2. Stir in tomatoes, garlic, oregano and basil. Place spinach on top of the chicken and cover.
3. Simmer until chicken is cooked through, approximately 15 more minutes.

Chicken Fricassee

Don't be intimidated by the ingredient list. This recipe is easier than it looks and well worth it!

Ingredients

1/4 cup arrowroot powder
1/2 tsp. Himalayan sea salt
1/2 tsp. fresh ground pepper
1 tsp. thyme
2 boneless skinless chicken breast
1 tbsp. extra virgin olive oil
10 clove garlic (minced)
2 cups tomatoes (chopped)
2 tbsp. tomato paste
1/4 cup water
1 can artichoke hearts (drained and rinsed)
1/2 cup Kalamata olives (pitted and chopped)
1/2 cup fresh basil (chopped)
3 tbsp. fresh oregano (chopped)
6 cups baby spinach (chopped)
2 tbsp. apple cider vinegar

Instructions

1. Place arrowroot powder, sea salt, black pepper and dried thyme into a shallow dish and gently mix together with a fork. Add the chicken pieces and toss chicken to coat with arrowroot mixture.
2. Heat olive oil in a large skillet over medium heat. Add chicken pieces and lightly sauté for about 5 minutes, moving the chicken around to cook on all sides.
3. Add the crushed garlic and continue to cook for about another minute, keeping everything moving in the pan.
4. Add the diced tomatoes, apple cider vinegar, tomato paste, and water. Stir to mix everything together. Then add the artichoke hearts and Kalamata olives, basil and oregano. Mix well, cover and simmer for 25 to 35 minutes over low heat, stirring occasionally.
5. Then add the spinach and cook for about another 10 minutes. Remove from heat and add salt and pepper to taste. Garnish with chopped fresh basil and oregano.

Chicken Korma

This is unbelievably good! Add extra Chili paste for a hotter version.

Ingredients

4		boneless skinless chicken breast
2		onions (finely sliced)
1	tbsp.	fresh ginger (chopped)
1	can	chickpeas (drained and rinsed)
1⁄2	cup	cilantro (chopped)
1	tbsp.	extra virgin olive oil
1⁄2	tsp.	mild chili paste
1	can	coconut milk
1⁄4	cup	almonds (sliced)
2	tbsp.	unsweetened shredded coconut
		Himalaya salt and pepper (to taste)
1		lemon
2 1⁄2	cups	brown rice (cooked)
1	cup	coconut yogurt

Instructions

1. Cut the chicken into 1 inch pieces.
2. Place olive oil in a large, deep pan on medium high heat. And add the onions, ginger and cilantro.
3. Stir often and cook for 8-10 minutes.
4. Add the chili paste, coconut milk, sliced almond, chick peas, coconut and chicken.
5. Add 3/4 cup water to pan and stir.
6. Bring to a boil, then reduce heat, cover and simmer for about 30 minutes.
7. Add extra water if necessary.
8. Season with salt and pepper.
9. Squeeze lemon over top and serve over brown rice. Dollop some yogurt over top if desired.

Chicken Piccata

A lighter version of a traditional favorite.

Ingredients

4		boneless, skinless chicken breasts (1/4 inch thick)
3	tsp.	extra virgin olive oil (divided)
2	clove	garlic (minced)
1	cup	chicken stock
1	tbsp.	lemon juice
2	tbsp.	capers (coarsely chopped)
1	tbsp.	parsley (chopped)
1⁄4	cup	brown rice flour (or other gluten free flour)

Instructions

1. Reserve 1 tablespoon flour for later use. In a shallow dish, combine remaining flour with salt and pepper. Dredge chicken in flour to coat.
2. In a medium skillet, add 1 teaspoon oil and heat at medium high. Add chicken and cook 2 to 3 minutes per side. Remove chicken from pan and set aside.
3. Add 2 tsp oil to the skillet along with garlic and reserved flour. Heat for about 1 minute and then add chicken stock, lemon juice and capers.
4. Boil this mixture over medium heat and simmer until sauce thickens.
5. Add chicken back to pan with the sauce and simmer for a couple more minutes. Stir parsley into pan and serve.

Chicken Roll Ups

A bundle of goodness all rolled up.

Ingredients

2		Portobello mushrooms (thinly sliced)
		Himalayan salt and pepper (to taste)
4		boneless, skinless chicken breasts (pounded to 1/8-inch thickness)
2	tbsp.	parsley (chopped and divided)
1	cup	tomato sauce
2	tsp.	extra virgin olive oil
1⁄2	cup	vegan Daiya mozzarella cheese

Instructions

1. Preheat oven to 350°F.
2. Place mushrooms on a baking sheet, drizzle with olive oil and bake for 15 minutes, until mushrooms are softened. Remove and set aside.
3. Season chicken breasts with salt and pepper, place mushrooms in the middle of each breast, top with 2 tbsp. of cheese and 1 tsp parsley.
4. Fold in sides of chicken then, roll chicken breast, enclosing filling. Secure rolls with toothpick or kitchen twine.
5. Heat tomato sauce in a saucepan until hot, set aside and keep warm.
6. Heat olive oil in a large skillet over medium heat. Place rolls in pan and cook on all sides until golden brown. Transfer chicken rolls to a baking dish and place in oven for 10 minutes.
7. Slice each roll in half, pour tomato sauce over each breast and sprinkle remaining parsley over top.

Chicken with Asparagus and Almond Pesto

Delicious grilled chicken with a twisted pesto sauce.

Ingredients

1	lb.	asparagus (trimmed)
2	cups	grape tomatoes
3	tbsp.	extra virgin olive oil
1⁄2	cup	almonds (sliced)
1⁄4	cup	fresh basil leaves
		Himalayan sea salt and pepper
4		boneless, skinless, chicken breasts

Instructions

1. Preheat the oven to 425°F.
2. Arrange the asparagus on half of a rimmed baking sheet and the tomatoes on the other half. Drizzle with olive oil and season with sea salt and pepper and toss to coat. Roast for about 20 minutes or until the asparagus is bright green and the tomatoes have collapsed. Let cool and remove the tips from the roasted asparagus and set aside.
3. Reserve 1 tbsp. of the almonds and place the rest in a food processor. Roughly chop the asparagus bottoms and place these in the food processor as well along with the basil and 3 tbsp. olive oil. Pulse until a paste forms. Season with salt and pepper.
4. Heat grill. Spread a spoonful of the pesto on top of each chicken breast. Grill until no longer pink inside and juice runs clear.
5. Mix the asparagus tops and tomatoes and evenly distribute among plates and serve with the grilled chicken breasts. You may wish to spread any leftover pesto over the chicken as well.

Chicken with Lemon and Olives

A combination of orange juice, lemon juice and green olives create a delicious sauce for this chicken dish.

Ingredients

2		oranges (juiced)
2		lemons (juiced)
2	tbsp.	raw honey
1	tsp.	cumin
6	clove	garlic (chopped)
4		chicken leg quarters (skinned)
1/2	tsp.	Himalayan sea salt
1/2	tsp.	pepper
14		pimiento stuffed green olives (halved)
1		lemon (thinly sliced)
1/4	cup	fresh parsley (chopped)
2	tbsp.	extra virgin olive oil

Instructions

1. Preheat oven to 400°F.
2. Combine the first 5 ingredients. Pour this over the chicken and let sit for 15 minutes. Pour remaining marinade into a 13 x 9 baking dish.
3. Heat 1 tbsp. olive oil in a large skillet over medium heat. Add the chicken and cook on each side until browned.
4. Place chicken in dish and sprinkle with salt and pepper. Top this with olives and lemon slices. Put in the oven and bake for 40 minutes.
5. Top with parsley and serve.

Coconut Chicken Skewers

So, sooo yummy!

Ingredients

1	cup	coconut milk
2	tbsp.	raw honey (divided)
1	tbsp.	lime juice
2	tbsp.	gluten free tamari (divided)
1⁄2	tsp.	cayenne pepper
1	tsp.	fresh ginger (grated or chopped)
4		boneless, skinless chicken breasts (cut into 1 inch strips)
2⁄3	cup	organic natural peanut butter
2	cloves	garlic (minced)
1 1⁄2	tbsp.	lemon juice
1⁄2	tsp.	crushed red pepper flakes

Instructions

1. Combine first 6 ingredients (1 tbsp. raw honey and 1 tbsp. gluten free tamari) in a medium bowl and mix well.
2. Marinate the chicken in the above mixture for at least 30 minutes. Remove from marinade. Do not discard the marinade
3. Preheat grill.
4. Thread the chicken on skewers and grill for 3 to 5 minutes. Brush the chicken with marinade and turn occasionally as the chicken cooks.

Peanut Sauce:

1. In a pot combine 1 cup water, peanut butter and garlic.
2. Cook over medium heat until the sauce boils and thickens. Remove from heat.
3. Stir in the remaining 1 tbsp. raw honey, lemon juice, tamari and red pepper flakes.

Coconut Lime Chicken

Chicken dippers that will leave you and the kids wanting more!

Ingredients

4 boneless, skinless chicken breasts (cut into cubes)
1⁄2 cup coconut milk (divided)
1⁄2 cup lime juice (divided)
1 tbsp. extra virgin olive oil
1⁄4 cup gluten free tamari (divided)
6 tbsp. almond butter
1 tbsp. raw honey
2 cloves garlic (minced)

Instructions

1. Place chicken pieces in a bowl and cover with 2 tablespoons coconut milk, 2 tablespoons lime juice and 2 tablespoons gluten free tamari. Stir to coat and marinate for 20 minutes.
2. In a medium skillet, heat olive oil over medium heat. Add chicken pieces and cooked until cooked through.
3. Place remaining ingredients in a bowl and whisk together until thickened and well combined.
4. Serve chicken pieces with dipping sauce.

Curried Chicken, Potatoes and Peas

All mixed up in a coconut curry sauce. This is a one pot wonder for sure!

Ingredients

3		boneless, skinless chicken breasts (sliced 3/4 inch thick)
		Himalayan sea salt and pepper (to taste)
2	tbsp.	extra virgin olive oil
1/2	cup	onion (chopped)
1	tbsp.	fresh ginger (minced)
1	tsp.	jalapeno (minced)
1	tbsp.	sweet curry powder
1	cup	chicken stock
1		red potato (peeled, cut into small chunks)
1	can	coconut milk
1/2	cup	frozen peas
2	tbsp.	cilantro (chopped)

Instructions

1. Season the chicken with salt and pepper. Heat the oil in a medium skillet over medium heat. Cook the chicken until cooked through and lightly browned. Remove from the skillet and keep warm.
2. Return the skillet to heat, adding a teaspoon of olive oil if needed, and add the onion, ginger and jalapeno. Sauté until the vegetables soften and then add the curry powder and sauté for another 30 seconds.
3. Pour the chicken stock into the skillet and add the potato and 1/2 tsp salt. Simmer and cook, partly covered until the potato is tender, about 7 minutes.
4. Add the coconut milk and peas. Simmer a few minutes until the sauce is a bit thickened.
5. Add the chicken to the sauce, toss to coat and serve sprinkled with cilantro.

Garlic Chicken Stir Fry

A tasty way to get in your vegetables.

For a lower carb version choose to leave out the rice or substitute cauliflower rice instead.

Cauliflower Rice
Grate 1/2 head of cauliflower into rice like pieces.

Add to a skillet with 1 tsp coconut or extra virgin olive oil and sauté for 5 minutes. Season with sea salt and ground black pepper.

Ingredients

2	tsp.	extra virgin olive oil
1		zucchini (sliced)
1	cup	red bell pepper (diced)
1	cup	yellow bell pepper (diced)
1/2	cup	fresh pineapple (diced)
2	tbsp.	ginger root (peeled and minced)
3	clove	garlic (minced)
1/2	cup	vegetable stock
3		boneless, skinless chicken breasts
2	cups	spinach
2	cup	brown rice (cooked-optional)
1/2	tsp.	red pepper flakes
1	tbsp.	gluten free tamari

Instructions

1. Preheat a grill. Sprinkle the chicken breasts with salt and pepper. Place on grill and cook until no longer pink inside.
2. In a large skillet heat the olive oil over medium heat. Add the zucchini, peppers, pineapple and garlic. Cook until the vegetables are tender. Add the vegetable stock if necessary.
3. Stir in the chicken and cook for another few minutes. Add the red pepper flakes and tamari sauce.
4. Add the spinach and cook until wilted. Serve over brown rice or cauliflower rice.

Ginger Chicken Stir-Fry

So simple and so tasty! I love using left over chicken for this recipe on busy nights.

Ingredients

2		boneless chicken breasts (cut into bite size pieces)
1	tbsp.	extra virgin olive oil
1	clove	garlic
1	tbsp.	ginger (finely chopped)
1		onion (cut into small wedges)
1		red pepper (cut into thin strips)
1	cup	broccoli (cut into small pieces)
1	cup	chicken stock
1	tsp.	arrow root powder
1	tbsp.	Bragg's Liquid Aminos (Gluten free Tamari can also be substituted)

Instructions

1. Heat oil in large skillet or wok and add chicken. Cook for approximately 5 minutes. Remove and set aside.
2. Add garlic, ginger, onion, peppers, broccoli and 1/4 cup chicken stock to the skillet. Sauté for 5 minutes.
3. Meanwhile, mix the arrowroot powder into the remaining 1/4 cup chicken stock and Bragg's sauce.
4. Return chicken to skillet, add Bragg's mixture and boil and then turn to simmer for 10 minutes.
5. Stir until the sauce thickens.

Goat Cheese Stuffed Chicken Breasts

Stuffed with goat cheese and sautéed onions, these are bursting with flavor.

Ingredients

3	tsp.	extra virgin olive oil (divided)
1 1/4	cup	sweet onion (thinly sliced)
1/2	tsp.	sea salt (divided)
1/4	tsp.	pepper
3/4	cup	goat cheese (crumbled)
2	cups	spinach
2	tbsp.	flat leaf parsley (chopped)
1/4	cup	fresh basil (chopped)
4		boneless, skinless chicken breasts
1 1/2	cups	chicken stock

Instructions

1. Heat 2 tsp. oil in a large skillet over medium heat. Add onions, 1/4 tsp. sea salt and pepper to pan; cook 12 minutes, stirring frequently. Cover, reduce heat, and cook another 8 minutes, stirring occasionally. Uncover and cook 5 minutes or until golden, stirring occasionally. This gives the onions a delicious caramelized taste. Add the spinach and cook until it begins to wilt. Cool slightly.
2. Combine onion mixture, 1/4 teaspoon salt, cheese, parsley and basil in a small bowl and mix.
3. Cut a horizontal slit through thickest portion of each chicken breast half to form a pocket; stuff 1 1/2 tbsp. cheese mixture into each pocket. Sprinkle chicken evenly with sea salt.
4. Return pan to medium-high heat. Coat pan with 1 teaspoon olive oil. Add chicken to pan; sauté 5 minutes; turn chicken over. Cover, reduce heat, and cook 10 minutes or until chicken is done.
5. Remove chicken from pan; let stand 10 minutes. Add chicken stock to pan; bring to a boil, scraping pan to loosen browned bits. Cook until reduced by half and serve with chicken.

Grilled Apple Chicken

Sweet and tangy, these are delicious grilled up!

Ingredients

1/2	cup	unsweetened apple juice
1/3	cup	lemon juice
2	cloves	garlic
1	tsp.	ginger root (peeled and minced)
3	tsp.	extra virgin olive oil
3	tbsp.	gluten free tamari
3	tbsp.	raw honey
4		boneless, skinless chicken breasts

Instructions

1. Combine the first 7 ingredients in a small bowl. Set aside 1/3 cup of the juice mixture.
2. Add oil to the remaining juice and pour into a reseal able bag. Add the chicken, seal the bag and refrigerate for at least an hour.
3. Heat grill, drain chicken and discard marinade. Grill over medium heat for about 6 minutes each side or until juices are clear. Baste occasionally with reserved juice mixture.

Grilled Chicken with Citrus Salsa

You'll love the fresh Zip and Zang of this chicken. Great for a hot summers night.

Ingredients

1/4	cup	lime juice (divided)
3	tbsp.	extra virgin olive oil (divided)
1		jalapeno pepper (diced)
4		boneless, skinless chicken breasts
		Himalaya sea salt and pepper (to taste)
1		orange (peeled and cut into small pieces)
1		pink grapefruit (peeled and cut into small pieces)
4		green onions (thinly sliced)
10		cherry tomatoes (halved)
1/2		fresh orange (zested and juiced)
1/2		lime (zested)
1/4	cup	fresh cilantro (chopped)
2		tomatillos (diced)
4	cups	salad greens

Instructions

1. Preheat grill.
2. In a shallow dish, combine 3 tbsp. lime juice and 2 tbsp. olive oil. Rub the chicken with salt and pepper and add to the marinade. Marinate for at least 20 minutes.
3. In a medium bowl, combine the citrus fruits, green onion, tomatoes, remaining 1 tbsp. lime juice, olive oil, orange and lime zest, jalapeno, cilantro and tomatillos. Mix and set aside.
4. Remove the chicken from the marinade. Cook on a hot grill on each side until cooked through.
5. Remove from the grill and let stand a few minutes.
6. Divide the salad greens among 4 plates, slice the chicken and arrange on top of the greens. Spoon salsa over each salad and serve.

Grilled Greek Chicken

Try this simple grilled chicken anytime of the year. Pair it with mixed wild greens for a lighter meal or Coconut Cardamom Yams for a heavier meal.

Ingredients

4		boneless, skinless chicken breasts
2	tsp.	oregano
2	tbsp.	extra virgin olive oil
2	tsp.	dried parsley
2	clove	garlic (minced)
1		lemon (juiced)
		Himalayan salt and pepper (to taste)

Instructions

1. Make small cuts in the chicken breasts and place in a sealable container.
2. In a small bowl combine lemon juice, olive oil, oregano, parsley and garlic. Pour this mixture over the chicken breasts and marinate for at least 30 minutes.
3. Place chicken on heated grill and occasionally brush with left over marinade until no longer pink inside.

Honey Chicken Kabobs

Deliciously made with all "good for you" ingredients! Great for a summer BBQ.

Ingredients

1 1⁄2	lb.	boneless skinless chicken breast (cut into bite size pieces)
2		zucchini (sliced into bite size pieces)
1		bell pepper (cut into bite size pieces)
1		red onion (cut into 8 wedges)
2	tbsp.	lemon juice
1	tbsp.	raw honey
1	tbsp.	extra virgin olive oil
1	tsp.	Dijon mustard
1	clove	garlic (crushed)
2	tsp.	fresh thyme (1/2 tsp dry thyme can be substituted)
		Himalayan salt and pepper (to taste)
16		cherry tomatoes
8		wooden or metal skewers (If using wooden, then soak in cold water for 10 minutes to prevent burning)

Instructions

1. In a large mixing bowl, combine lemon juice, honey, olive oil, mustard and crushed garlic. Stir in thyme, salt, and pepper. Add chicken, zucchini, bell pepper and onion. Toss until well coated. Let marinate in the fridge for 1 hour.
2. Preheat grill to medium. Thread the chicken and vegetables onto the skewers. Save the marinade mixture.
3. Grill on medium. Turn the kebabs every few minutes to make sure they cook evenly. Brush with reserve marinade mix every few minutes as well. Grill until juices run clear when chicken is pierced with a knife, approximately 10 to 12 minutes.

Mango Coconut Chicken with Black Beans

The combination of mint, coriander and coconut makes this recipe uniquely delicious.

Ingredients

1	tbsp.	extra virgin olive oil
4		boneless, skinless chicken breasts (cut into strips)
2	tsp.	ground coriander
1/2	cup	chicken stock
1	cup	coconut milk
1		mango (peeled and cut into 1/2 inch pieces)
2	can	black beans (rinsed)
2	tbsp.	lime juice
4	tbsp.	fresh mint (chopped)

Instructions

1. Heat the oil in a large skillet over high heat. Add the chicken and cook until browned on both sides.
2. Add the coriander and stir. Add the chicken broth and reduce heat. Cook for 3 more minutes. Transfer the chicken to a plate.
3. Add the coconut milk to the skillet and increase the heat. Boil and reduce by half.
4. Stir in the mango and cook until heated through. Return the chicken to the skillet, season with salt and pepper and remove from heat.
5. Meanwhile, simmer the black beans over low heat in a medium saucepan. Stir in the lime juice and 3 tbsp. mint.
6. Divide the beans among your plates and top with the chicken and remaining 1 tbsp. mint.

Mediterranean Chicken

A taste of the Mediterranean on your dinner table. Serve over brown rice, quinoa or shredded cabbage for a complete meal.

This sauce can easily be made ahead of time (the flavours only get better) and kept in the fridge for up 2 weeks. It can also be stored in the freezer for up to 6 months.

Ingredients

3	tbsp.	extra virgin olive oil (divided)
1		red onion (minced)
2	cups	plum tomatoes (drained)
1⁄4	cup	chicken stock
2	clove	garlic (minced)
1⁄2	tsp.	dried basil
1⁄2	tsp.	dried oregano
1⁄4	tsp.	thyme
1⁄4	tsp.	bay leaf (finely crumbled)
1⁄4	tsp.	coriander seed
1⁄4	tsp.	fennel seed
4		boneless chicken breasts

Instructions

To make the sauce:

1. Heal 1 tablespoon olive oil in large skillet over medium heat.
2. Add onion and sauté until golden. Stir in remaining ingredients (except chicken) and simmer for 30 minutes. Remove from heat.

To make chicken:

1. Heat 2 tbsp. olive oil in a large skillet over medium-high heat. Add chicken and sauté until cooked through, about 3 minutes on each side.
2. Transfer the chicken to plates and divide sauce among pieces.

Red Thai Curry Chicken

A simple Thai dish that is sure to please. This Thai sauce can be made for a variety of other dishes of your choice. Feel free to add any other vegetables such as snow peas or sliced zucchini.

Ingredients

2	tbsp.	coconut oil
6		boneless, skinless chicken breasts (cut into strips)
3	cloves	garlic (minced)
5		green onions (chopped)
1		red bell pepper (sliced)
1⁄2	cup	mushrooms (sliced)
1	can	bamboo shoots (drained)
1	can	coconut milk
2	tbsp.	red curry paste (can be adjusted for desired heat)
3⁄4	tsp.	rice vinegar
1⁄4	cup	cilantro (chopped)
3⁄4	tsp.	gluten free tamari

Instructions

1. In a small bowl, mix together the coconut milk, curry paste, vinegar and tamari and set aside.
2. In a large skillet, heat the coconut oil. Add the chicken and cook until the sides are browned. Transfer to a plate and set aside.
3. In the skillet, add the garlic, green onion, peppers, mushrooms and bamboo shoots. Cook for 3-4 minutes.
4. Add the chicken and the curry sauce. Stir, making sure the chicken is partially covered in the liquid.
5. Reduce the heat and cover. Stir occasionally for about 10 minutes or until the chicken is completely cooked through.
6. Sprinkle with cilantro and serve.

Roasted Garlic Chicken with Sweet Potatoes

The perfect meal for a cold winters night. The roasted garlic and rosemary make the dish!

Ingredients

4		boneless, skinless chicken breasts
3		sweet potatoes (peeled and thickly sliced)
3	tbsp.	lemon juice
2	tbsp.	extra virgin olive oil
3	tbsp.	fresh rosemary (chopped)
1	tsp.	sea salt
2		whole heads of garlic (unpeeled)

Instructions

1. Preheat oven to 425°F.
2. Combine potatoes, chicken, lemon juice, 1 1/2 tbsp. olive oil, rosemary, salt and pepper in a bowl and toss to coat.
3. In a glass baking dish, arrange potatoes in a single layer. Place chicken over top of the potatoes.
4. Trim tops from garlic head and brush with remaining 1/2 tbsp. olive oil. Place these in glass dish along with the chicken and potatoes.
5. Place dish in oven and roast, occasionally basting, for about an hour, or until juices run clear when chicken is pierced.
6. Divide chicken and potatoes evenly and squeeze the garlic onto individual servings.

Rosemary and Dijon Roasted Chicken

The perfect Sunday evening meal for the whole family!

Ingredients

1		whole roasting chicken
1	tbsp.	Dijon mustard
3		sprigs fresh rosemary
1		lemon (zested and juiced)
4	cloves	garlic (peeled and cut into 1/2 inch pieces)
1		onion (quartered)
		Himalayan sea salt and pepper (to taste)
1⁄4	cup	raw honey
2	cups	carrots (chopped)
2	cups	sweet potato (chopped)
2	cups	green beans (trimmed and halved)

Instructions

1. Preheat oven to 375°F. Rinse the chicken and season it with salt and pepper
2. Place the chicken in a large roasting pan.
3. Chop two sprigs of the rosemary. In a small bowl, mix together Dijon mustard, honey, chopped rosemary, lemon juice and lemon zest.
4. Place the remaining sprig of rosemary, a lemon half, the onion quarters and garlic in the cavity of the bird. Using a pastry brush, coat the outside of the bird with the lemon honey glaze.
5. Layer the vegetables around the chicken.
6. Place the roasting pan in the oven and baste the chicken every 15 minutes with any remaining glaze. Roast for about an hour or until juices run clear.

Slow Cooker Chicken Enchiladas

For a no fuss meal time, prepare this the night before, place it in the crock pot, refrigerate and simply turn it on in the morning and go!

Ingredients

1	tbsp.	extra virgin olive oil
6	cloves	garlic (minced)
1		onion (chopped)
2		green bell peppers (chopped)
24	oz.	diced tomatoes
4	oz.	green chilies
1	tsp.	cumin
		sea salt (to taste)
1⁄2	tsp.	cayenne pepper
4		boneless, skinless chicken breasts (cut into pieces)
2	can	pinto beans (rinsed and drained)
5	oz.	sliced black olives (drained and rinsed)
1 1⁄2	cup	organic frozen corn
1	cup	Daiya mozzarella cheese (shredded)
6		organic corn tortillas

Instructions

1. Heat the oil in a large skillet over medium heat. Add the garlic and onions and sauté.
2. Add the bell pepper and cook a few more minutes. Stir in the tomatoes, chilies and cumin. Season with salt and cayenne pepper.
3. Spoon 1/4 of the sauce onto the bottom of the slow cooker. Follow that with 1/3 of the chicken, beans, olives, corn and Daiya cheese. Top with 2 tortillas.
4. Repeat steps 3 times.
5. Cover and cook on low about 4 or 4 1/2 hours, or until bubbly throughout.

Spicy Chicken Lettuce Wraps

These lettuce wraps are loaded with flavours and fun for the whole family to make!

Ingredients

1 1⁄2	lb.	boneless skinless chicken breast (sliced)
3	tbsp.	arrow root powder
4	tbsp.	sesame oil (divided in half)
2	tbsp.	extra virgin olive oil
1⁄4	cup	green onion (thinly sliced)
3	tbsp.	ginger (minced)
1	tbsp.	jalapeno (finely chopped)
1⁄2	tbsp.	garlic (minced)
8	oz.	water chestnuts (rinsed and chopped)
1	cup	baby bok choy (thinly sliced)
1	cup	tamari sauce (divided (3/4 cups and 3 tablespoons))
1 1⁄4	cup	rice wine vinegar (divided (1 cup, 1/4 cup))
3	tbsp.	cilantro (chopped)
2		iceberg lettuce heads (washed and separated)
1⁄4	cup	sesame seeds
1		lime (zested and juiced)

Instructions

1. Sprinkle arrowroot evenly over chicken.
2. In a large skillet, heat 1 tbsp. sesame oil and 1 tbsp. olive oil. Add the chicken and cook until cooked through. About 5 minutes. Transfer chicken to a plate and set aside.
3. Add the remaining oil to the skillet along with the green onion, ginger, jalapeno and garlic. Cook over medium heat for a couple of minutes.
4. Add the water chestnuts, bok choy and 3 tablespoons tamari sauce. Cook, stirring often, until the bok choy wilts, 4-5 minutes.
5. Return the chicken to the skillet and cook until heated through.
6. Transfer chicken to a serving plate. Whisk the remaining arrowroot into the liquid still in the skillet and cook, continually stirring until it thickens. Pour this sauce over the chicken.
7. Sprinkle cilantro over chicken. Scoop a few tbsp. of chicken mixture into each lettuce leaf and loosely roll up. Serve with dipping sauce.

Dipping Sauce

Place 1/4 cup sesame seeds, 3/4 cup tamari sauce, 1/4 cup rice vinegar 1 lime, zested and juiced and 2 tbsp. sesame oil in a sealable container and shake vigorously. This can be refrigerated for up to 7 days.

Spicy Garlic Chicken Crunch

Crushed crispy rice cereal makes a delicious alternative to breadcrumbs for that little crunch you love!

For a gluten free alternative to panko, pulse 1/2 cup crisp rice cereal through a food processor until consistency of bread crumbs.

Ingredients

4		boneless, skinless chicken breasts
1/2	tsp.	sea salt
1/4	tsp.	black pepper
2	clove	garlic (minced)
1/2	tsp.	oregano
1/4	cup	lemon juice
1/4	cup	honey
2	tsp.	tabasco sauce
1	tsp.	lemon zest
2	tbsp.	extra virgin olive oil
1/2	cup	crushed gluten free Crispy Rice cereal

Instructions

1. Season the chicken breasts with salt and pepper.
2. Mix together the crushed cereal, garlic and oregano and place in a shallow dish or pie pan. Dredge both sides of the chicken in the mixture.
3. Mix the lemon juice, honey, tabasco sauce and lemon zest in a small bowl and set aside.
4. Heat the olive oil in a skillet over medium heat. Add the chicken and cook until browned on both sides and cooked through. Place chicken on a plate and set aside.
5. Add the lemon honey mixture to the skillet and cook until it thickens, less than a minute. Return the chicken to the skillet and turn to coat.

Thai Chicken Curry

Another delicious version of chicken curry. This is easily frozen for a great, ready to go meal.

The marinade takes a few minutes to prepare. If time permits, prepare marinade in the morning or the evening before and let it sit in the fridge during the day for an easy, no mess dinner.

Ingredients

4		boneless, skinless chicken breasts
1	can	coconut milk
4		shallots (peeled)
6	clove	garlic (peeled and minced)
2	tbsp.	fresh ginger chopped
2	tbsp.	fish sauce
3	tbsp.	organic peanut butter
1	tbsp.	curry powder
1	tsp.	crushed red chili flakes
1	tsp.	coriander
1	tsp.	cumin
1	tsp.	turmeric
1/4	tsp.	pepper
2	tbsp.	raw honey
1	tbsp.	gluten free tamari
1/2	cup	cilantro
2	cup	spinach
1	cup	zucchini (diced)

Instructions

1. Cut chicken into pieces and place in a baking dish.
2. Place remaining ingredients (except cilantro, spinach and zucchini) in a food processor and pulse until smooth and creamy.
3. Cover the chicken with the curry marinade. Cover and refrigerate for at least a half hour but up to 24 hours.
4. Preheat oven to 400°F. Place chicken in oven and bake for 30 minutes.
5. Sauté spinach and zucchini in 1 tbsp. olive oil for about 5 minutes.
6. Remove the chicken from the oven and mix in sautéed veggies.
7. Garnish with cilantro and serve

Southeast Fried Rice

A fantastic one dish wonder. This is great for left-over rice or make the rice the night before for greater ease.

Ingredients

1	tbsp.	fish sauce
1	tbsp.	gluten free tamari sauce
1	tbsp.	lime juice
1	tsp	chili paste
		Himalayan sea salt (to taste)
2		eggs (beaten)
1		green onion (chopped)
2	tbsp.	extra virgin olive oil
2 1/2	cups	brown rice (cooked and cooled)
1/4	cup	shallots (sliced)
2		boneless, skinless chicken breasts (cut into bite size pieces)
2	cups	broccoli (cut into bite size pieces)
1	cup	red bell pepper (julienne cut)
2	cloves	garlic (minced)

Instructions

1. In a small bowl combine fish sauce, tamari, lime juice, chili paste and a dash of sea salt.
2. In a large nonstick skillet, heat 1/2 tbsp. of the olive oil over medium heat. Add the rice and stir fry for a couple of minutes. Transfer the rice to a large bowl.
3. Heat 1 1/2 tbsp. olive oil in the pan and add the shallots, green onion, garlic, broccoli and bell pepper and sauté until tender. Add the chicken and stir fry until browned and no longer pink inside. Add the tamari mixture and bring to a boil. Reduce heat and simmer for 1 minute or until liquid thickens.
4. Add the chicken and vegetable mixture to the rice and mix to combine. Set aside.
5. Add the eggs to the pan and cook for 30 second or just until the egg is set. Transfer the eggs to a cutting board and chop. Place the egg, chicken, rice and vegetables together in the pan and heat through. Serve.

Clean Cabbage Rolls

Even better than your Grandma made them!

Ingredients

1	cup	brown rice (cooked)
1		medium head green cabbage
1	lb.	lean ground turkey
1		yellow onion (chopped, divided)
3		roma tomatoes (diced)
2	tsp.	oregano (divided)
2	tsp.	cinnamon (divided)
1/4	tsp.	cayenne pepper (divided)
1/2	cup	gluten free bread crumbs
2		egg whites
6	oz.	tomato paste
1/2	cup	mushrooms (sliced)
1/4	cup	apple cider vinegar
1	tbsp.	thyme
		Himalayan sea salt and pepper (to taste)

Instructions

1. Fill a large pot with water and boil over medium heat. Remove from heat and put cabbage head in a colander and pour hot water over cabbage.
2. Remove 8-9 leaves of cabbage and set aside.
3. In a large skillet, sauté turkey until no longer pink. Add onion (saving 2 tbsp. for sauce) and sauté an additional 3 minutes. Add tomatoes, 1 tsp oregano, 1 tsp cinnamon and 1/8 tsp cayenne and sauté another couple of minutes and remove from heat.
4. In a large bowl, mix cooked rice, bread crumbs and egg whites. Combine this with turkey mixture.
5. Preheat oven to 350°F.
6. Stuff cabbage rolls: Place 1/2 cup turkey mixture in the middle of a cabbage leaf, fold ends into the middle, roll and seal with a toothpick.
7. In a medium sauce pan add reserved 2 tbsp. onion and sauté until translucent.
8. Stir in tomato paste, mushrooms, 1/2 cup water, vinegar, remaining 1 teaspoon oregano and cinnamon, 1/8 tsp cayenne and thyme. Season with salt and pepper.
9. Cook for about 2 minutes and spread 1 to 2 tbsp. sauce on the bottom of a casserole dish, place cabbage rolls on top and spread remaining sauce over the top of the cabbage rolls.
10. Cover dish and bake for about 45 minutes.

Coconut Crusted Turkey Strips

Sure to be a family favourite! Serve with raw veggies and hummus for a quick weeknight meal.

Ingredients

2		egg whites
2	tsp.	sesame oil
1/2	cup	coconut flakes
2	tbsp.	sesame seeds
		Himalayan sea salt and black pepper
1 1/2	lb.	turkey breast tenderloin (cut into strips)
1/2	cup	Gluten free crispy rice cereal (crushed)

Instructions

1. Preheat oven to 425°F.
2. Whisk egg white and oil in a shallow dish. In another bowl, combine coconut, cereal, sesame seeds and salt and a dash of pepper.
3. Dip the turkey strips in the egg mixture and then into the coconut mixture.
4. Place the turkey on baking sheets and bake for 5-7 minutes on each side or until golden brown.
5. Remove from oven and enjoy!

Not So Spaghetti and Meatballs

All the fun of an old time favourite with none of the carbs!

Ingredients

1		spaghetti squash (large in size; baked)
1 1⁄2	lb.	lean ground turkey
5	clove	garlic (divided and minced)
1⁄2	tsp.	Himalayan sea salt
1		onion (chopped)
4		egg whites
2	tsp.	extra virgin olive oil (divided)
1	can	Organic Tomato Sauce (Or canned crushed tomatoes)
1	tsp.	dried basil
1	tsp.	dried oregano

Instructions

1. Cut squash in half and place in shallow baking dish with one-inch water. Bake for 1 hour at 350°F or microwave for 10-12 minutes or until fork tender.
2. Using a fork, remove the squash from the shell by scraping it from the top of the sides to the center. This will achieve the “spaghetti-like” strings.
3. Lightly sauté the onion and 3 cloves garlic in 1 tsp olive oil in nonstick pan for 4-5 minutes. Remove from pan and add to ground turkey with sea salt.
4. Mix turkey mixture with egg whites and form meatballs and bake at 350°F for approximately 30 minutes or until the internal temperature reaches 170°F.
5. In a medium skillet, heat remaining olive oil and sauté the remaining cloves of garlic. Add the tomato sauce, oregano and basil and simmer on low for 10 minutes.
6. Divide squash among plates, spoon desired amount of tomato sauce on top of the squash and top with meatballs.

Southwest Stuffed Turkey Breast

Healthy and tasty Southwestern flair!

Ingredients

1⁄3	cup	sun dried tomatoes (not packed in oil)
1 1⁄2	tsp.	oregano
1⁄2	tsp.	sea salt
1	tsp.	cumin
1⁄2	tsp.	coriander
1⁄4	tsp.	crushed red pepper flakes
1		onion (chopped)
1		green bell pepper (diced)
2	clove	garlic (minced)
1	tbsp.	extra virgin olive oil
1	cup	corn kernels
1		lime (zested)
1		boneless skinless turkey breast half (2 pounds)
1⁄4	cup	gluten free bread crumbs

Instructions

1. In a small bowl, place the sun dried tomatoes in a bowl with 2/3 cup boiling water. Cover and let stand for 5 minutes and drain, reserving 3 tbsp. of the liquid.
2. In another small bowl, combine the oregano, salt, cumin, coriander and red pepper flakes.
3. In a large skillet, heat the olive oil and sauté the sun dried tomatoes, onion, green pepper and garlic until tender.
4. Stir in the corn and seasonings and remove from heat. Stir in the bread crumbs, reserved liquid, and lime zest.
5. Cover the turkey breast with plastic wrap and flatten until it is 1/2 inch thick. Sprinkle the turkey with half of the lime and seasoning mixture and spread vegetable mixture up to the edges.
6. Roll up the turkey and tie with kitchen string. Sprinkle with the remaining lime/seasoning mixture. Place in a shallow roasting pan and cover loosely with foil.
7. Bake at 350°F for 1 hour. Remove the foil and bake another 20-30 minutes, basting with the pan drippings. Let cool and slice.

Turkey and Quinoa Mix Up

Black beans and corn give this a bit of a Mexican flair!

Ingredients

2	tbsp.	extra virgin olive oil
2	clove	garlic (minced)
1 1/2	tsp.	paprika
1	cup	quinoa
1 1/2	tsp.	cumin seeds
1 1/2	tsp.	coriander
1	tsp.	sea salt
1/2	tsp.	pepper
1	tsp.	cayenne pepper
1		onion (diced)
3		plum tomatoes (diced)
1		red bell pepper
1	can	black beans (rinsed and drained)
1	can	white kidney beans (rinsed and drained)
1		lime (juiced)
16	oz.	ground turkey breast
1	cup	organic non GMO frozen corn kernels

Instructions

1. Heat 1 tbsp. olive oil in a saucepan over medium heat. Sauté garlic and paprika, stirring, for about 30 seconds.
2. Add the quinoa and 2 cups of water. Bring to a boil. Reduce heat, cover and let simmer until quinoa is tender and no water remains, about 15 minutes.
3. In a large skillet, heat remaining 1 tbsp. olive oil over medium heat. Sauté the cumin, coriander, salt, pepper and cayenne for a couple of minutes.
4. Add the ground turkey (breaking into small pieces), the onion and pepper and cook until the turkey is no longer pink, about 20 minutes.
5. Add the tomatoes, beans and corn to the skillet and mix well. Cook for another 5 minutes.
6. Add the quinoa and lime juice and stir.

Turkey Meatloaf

Make a double batch and freeze for a later date. You won't regret it! Serve with Celery Root Smash Up.

Ingredients

1	lb.	ground turkey
1		egg (beaten)
3/4	cup	mushrooms (sautéed)
1/2	cup	carrot (shredded)
1		orange (squeezed)
2	tbsp.	dried parsley
2	tsp.	dried tarragon
1	tsp.	dried sage
1/4	cup	gluten free oats
½	cup	tomato sauce

Instructions

1. Preheat oven to 350°F.
2. Mix all ingredients (except tomato sauce) together in a medium bowl.
3. Pat into a loaf shape in a 9-inch pie plate or other flat dish. Top with tomato sauce.
4. Bake for approximately 35 minutes, uncovered.

Beef and Orange Soba Stir Fry

A quick, tasty dinner packed with nutrition.

Ingredients

1	tbsp.	extra virgin olive oil
1	lb.	lean steak round (sliced into strips)
1/2	cup	onion (diced)
2	cup	broccoli florets (cut into bite size pieces)
1/2		red bell pepper (julienne cut)
1		medium orange (juiced)
1	tbsp.	orange zest
2	clove	garlic (minced)
2	tsp.	arrowroot powder
12	oz.	gluten free soba noodles (black bean or mung bean noodles can also be used)
3	tbsp.	gluten free tamari sauce
2	tsp.	raw honey

Instructions

1. Cook noodles. Drain and set aside.
2. Heat large skillet over high heat for 1 minute. Reduce heat to medium high, mist pan with cooking spray and sauté steak for about 5 minutes or until cooked through. Remove steak, leaving juices in the pan.
3. Mist same pan again with cooking spray. Add onion, broccoli and pepper and sauté over medium high heat for about 5 minutes or until cooked through.
4. In a medium bowl, whisk together tamari, orange juice and zest, garlic and honey.
5. Add steak back to vegetables in pan and pour in tamari mixture. Sauté steak and vegetables over medium high heat for about 2 minutes, then whisk in arrowroot powder to thicken. Add noodles to pan and cook until warmed. Remove and serve.

Beef Biryani

A delicious Indian dish for the whole family. A fantastic way to use up leftover steak!

Ingredients

1⁄2	tsp.	Himalayan sea salt
1		onion (thinly sliced)
2	tbsp.	extra virgin olive oil
5	clove	garlic (thinly sliced)
1	cup	mango (cubed)
1⁄2	cup	frozen peas
16	oz.	sirloin tip (cut into strips)
1	cup	cherry tomatoes (halved)
1	tsp.	cumin
1⁄2	tsp.	cinnamon
1	tsp.	coriander
1	tsp.	turmeric
2	tsp.	ginger
1	cup	quinoa

Instructions

1. Bring 2 cups water to boil in a medium pot over high heat. Meanwhile combine spices in a small bowl and set aside. When water boils, add quinoa, stir, and reduce heat and cover. Simmer for 15 minutes and remove from heat.
2. When quinoa is cooking, sauté onion in olive oil in a large pan until onion is soft. Add garlic and stir often.
3. Add spice mixture, mango, peas and beef. Lower heat and make sure all ingredients are mixed well and cook for another 5-8 minutes.
4. Combine quinoa with beef mixture, top with tomatoes and serve.

Beef Fajitas

A make-it-yourself low carb sensation. This can be made with lettuce wraps for a quicker version. Serve with homemade guacamole if desired.

Ingredients

2	lb.	beef tenderloin
2		limes (juiced)
1		lemon (juiced)
1		orange (juiced)
4	tbsp.	pineapple juice (optional)
4	tbsp.	extra virgin olive oil (divided)
2	clove	garlic (minced)
1	tsp.	sea salt
1	tsp.	chili powder
1	dash	tabasco sauce
2		purple onions (thinly sliced)
1		red bell pepper (thinly sliced)
1		green bell pepper (thinly sliced)

Instructions

1. Toss all juices in a medium mixing bowl for marinade.
2. Add 1 tablespoon of olive oil, a dash of sea salt and black pepper, chili powder and tabasco sauce. Mix well.
3. Prepare Grain less wraps (recipe found in Sides) and wrap in foil and warm in oven at 200°F while you prepare the fajita mixture.
4. Divide the marinade and marinate the meat with half of the marinade for at least 30 minutes.
5. Toss vegetables with remaining marinade.
6. Heat 2 tablespoons olive oil in a large skillet over medium heat. Sauté meat until desired doneness and transfer to a plate. Place in oven with the tortillas to stay warm.
7. Add the remaining olive oil to the skillet and sauté the vegetables. Add the vegetables to the meat on a platter.
8. Place fajita mixture and Grain less wraps or large leaf lettuce cups on the table along with other desired toppings and have your friends and family create their own fajita.

Beef Rendang

An Indian inspired dish that's worth the wait!

Ingredients

1/2	cup	shallots (chopped)
1/3	cup	ginger (thinly sliced)
5	cloves	garlic (minced)
2	tbsp.	chili garlic sauce
1 1/2	tsp.	turmeric
1/2	tsp.	sea salt
1/4	tsp.	cinnamon
1/2	tsp.	cloves
1		serrano Chile (chopped)
1	can	coconut milk
2/3	cup	unsweetened coconut
1		lime (zested and juiced)
1 1/2	lb.	boneless chuck roast (trimmed and cut into 1 inch pieces)
14	oz.	beef stock

Instructions

1. Place the shallots, ginger, garlic, chili sauce, turmeric, sea salt, cinnamon, cloves and serrano Chile in a food processor. Add 1/4 cup of the coconut milk and process until smooth. Set aside.
2. Wipe out the food processor and place 1/4 cup coconut milk and flaked coconut in the food processor and process until a paste forms.
3. Place the shallots mixture in a large sauce pan over medium heat and cook for 1 minute. Stir in the remaining coconut milk and the lime juice and zest, the beef and the beef broth. Bring to a boil. Cover, reduce heat and simmer for about 1 1/2 hours.
4. Stir in the flaked coconut mixture and simmer another 5-10 minutes. Serve over greens or brown rice, if desired.

Bison Burgers

You can't go wrong with a tasty burger. Of course you can always use lean ground beef or venison for these. Serve with the Avocado and Corn Salad or Side Salad.

Ingredients

1	lb.	ground bison meat
1		onion (2 tbsp. chopped, the rest thinly sliced)
3	tbsp.	parsley (chopped)
1	tsp	Chile powder
1⁄2	tsp	Himalayan sea salt
2	tsp	extra virgin olive oil (divided)
1	cup	mushrooms (sliced)
1		small red bell pepper (sliced)
1		tomato (sliced)
4		gluten free buns (for a low carb version, wrap burger in large leaf lettuce)
4	leaves	Romaine lettuce

Instructions

1. In a large bowl combine bison, chopped onion, parsley, Chile powder salt and pepper. Mix until combined and form into patties.
2. Add 1 teaspoon oil to a nonstick skillet over medium heat. Add mushrooms and sauté until soft. Remove mushrooms from skillet and set aside.
3. Add remaining oil to skillet and sauté red pepper and remaining onion until tender and browned. Add to mushrooms.
4. Grill burgers over medium high heat to desired doneness.
5. Place patty on bun-if using, add sautéed vegetables, lettuce and tomato and enjoy!

Braised Beef and Root Vegetables

We use our crock pot at least once per week. I love coming home to a meal that is ready to serve!

For easy meal prep, have ingredients ready to go the night before and toss them in the crock pot in the morning. This will take minutes to prepare at meal time.

Ingredients

1		orange (zested and juiced)
1	lb.	beef chuck (trimmed and cut into bite sized chunks)
1/2	tsp.	Himalayan sea salt
1/2	cup	onion (chopped)
1	tsp.	cumin
1	tsp.	coriander
1	tsp.	cinnamon
1/4	tsp.	cayenne pepper
3	cloves	garlic (minced)
2	tbsp.	tomato paste
2	cups	vegetable broth
1		turnip (peeled and cut into chunks)
1	cup	parsnips (peeled and cut into chunks)
2		carrots (peeled and cut into chunks)
3		green onion (sliced)
1	cup	quinoa

Instructions

1. Place all ingredients except quinoa and green onion into a crock pot.
2. Cover and cook on low heat for 6-8 hours.
3. Bring 1 cup water to a boil. Stir in quinoa, cover and simmer for 15 minutes. Let sit for 5 to 10 minutes. Fluff with fork.
4. Serve beef over quinoa and sprinkle with green onion.

Flank Steak Roll

Slice this up to impress your family and friends. Serve with Garlic Mashers and Zucchini Ribbons.

Ingredients

1	tbsp.	pine nuts
2	tsp.	red wine vinegar
2	cloves	garlic (minced)
1/4	tsp.	sea salt
1/4	tsp.	red pepper flakes
1	lb.	flank steak (trimmed of fat)
6	cups	spinach leaves
1/4	cup	gluten free bread crumbs

Instructions

1. Preheat oven to 400°F.
2. Combine the bread crumbs, nuts, vinegar, garlic, salt and pepper flakes in a small bowl and set aside.
3. With a sharp knife, cut the steak almost in half horizontally, leaving an edge of about an inch in tact (this create 2 folds). Spread it open.
4. Evenly spread the bread crumb mixture over the steak. Arrange spinach on top of this.
5. Starting with the closest edge, roll steak up while pressing down. Tie with kitchen string.
6. Place steak in a baking dish and bake for about 40 minutes or until a meat thermometer reads 150 degrees.
7. When done, let it cool for a few minutes. Remove the string and cut crosswise into slices.

Peppered Beef with Spinach

To crack peppercorns, grind them under a hard object such as a glass measuring cup.

Ingredients

16	oz.	beef tenderloin filets
1/4	tsp.	sea salt
1/2	tsp.	black peppercorns (cracked)
2 1/2	tsp.	extra virgin olive oil (divided)
1/4	cup	low sodium beef broth
1	tbsp.	shallots (minced)
1/4	cup	almond milk or coconut milk
1	tbsp.	coarse ground mustard
1/2	cup	grape tomatoes (halved)
1	clove	garlic (minced)
6	cups	fresh spinach
1	tsp.	lemon juice
		Himalayan sea salt and pepper (to taste)

Instructions

1. Season the steaks with 1/4 tsp. salt and press peppercorns into one side of the filets.
2. Heat 2 tsp olive oil in a large sauté pan over medium heat and cook filets 4-5 minutes, depending on desired doneness. Remove steaks from pan and keep warm.
3. Remove the pan from heat and add beef broth and shallots. Simmer for a few minutes and add the milk and mustard.
4. Heat remaining 1/2 tsp. olive oil in a large nonstick skillet and sauté the tomatoes and garlic for a couple of minutes.
5. Add spinach to the skillet and sauté until wilted. Season mixture with lemon juice, salt and pepper.
6. Serve steaks with sauce and spinach mixture.

Rainbow Beef Stir Fry

A rainbow of colours from all of the delicious vegetables!

Ingredients

1	lb.	sirloin grilling steak (thinly sliced)
2	tbsp.	gluten free tamari
1	tbsp.	arrowroot powder
2	cloves	garlic
1	tbsp.	ginger root (minced)
1/2	tsp.	5 spice powder
1		red bell pepper (chopped in bite size pieces)
1		yellow bell pepper (chopped in bite size pieces)
3		green onion (chopped)
2	tbsp.	extra virgin olive oil
1/4	cup	beef stock
1	tsp.	sesame oil
1/4	cup	cilantro (chopped)
2	tbsp.	gluten free hoisin sauce

Instructions

1. In a medium bowl, toss together the beef, tamari, arrowroot powder, garlic, ginger and five spice powder. Let this stand for 20 minutes.
2. In a large skillet, heat the olive oil over medium heat and stir fry the beef mixture until browned. Transfer to a plate.
3. Add the red and yellow peppers and green onion to the skillet with 2 tbsp. of water. Cover and steam until peppers are tender crisp, about 3 minutes.
4. Place the beef back in the skillet, and stir in the beef stock, hoisin sauce and sesame oil. Simmer until thickened. Sprinkle with cilantro and serve.

Spicy Asian Marinated Flank Steak

An easy and tasty marinade makes this a sure to be favourite. This marinade can be quickly thrown together the night before for a quick, no fuss dinner the next day. Serve with Delicious Asparagus!

Ingredients

1	tbsp.	lime juice
1	tsp.	curry powder
1	tsp.	ground red pepper
2	tsp.	fresh ginger (peeled and minced)
1 1/2	tsp.	rice wine vinegar
1	tsp.	extra virgin olive oil
1	tsp.	sesame oil
8	oz.	crushed pineapple (drained)
4	clove	garlic (minced)
2	tbsp.	gluten free tamari
1	lb.	flank steak (trimmed)

Instructions

1. Combine first 10 ingredients in a large sealable bag. Add steak, seal and marinate up to 24 hours, turning occasionally.
2. Heat grill to medium heat.
3. Remove steak from bag and discard marinade. Place steaks on grill and grill for about 5 minutes on each side or until desired doneness.
4. Cut steak diagonally across grain into thin slices.

Sweet Potato Shepherd's Pie

Warms the heart and the soul.....

Ingredients

1		sweet potato (peeled and diced)
1	tbsp.	organic butter or Earth Balance *(This is a butter alternative found in the natural health aisle)*
1	cup	almond or coconut milk
1/4	tsp.	cinnamon
1/4	tsp.	nutmeg
1 1/2	tsp.	extra virgin olive oil
1		onion (chopped)
1	cup	leek (white part, thinly sliced)
1	cup	turnip (chopped)
1/2	cup	carrot (diced)
2	tsp.	fresh thyme (chopped)
2	tsp.	fresh rosemary (chopped)
1/4	cup	water
15	oz.	cannellini beans (drained and rinsed)
1	cup	low sodium vegetable broth

Instructions

To make Sweet Potato Topping:

1. Bring large pot of water to a boil. Add sweet potato, cover, and boil 10 minutes or until tender. Drain, and return to pot.
2. Mash with milk, butter or Earth Balance, cinnamon, and nutmeg; season with salt and pepper, if desired. Set aside.

To make Filling:

1. Heat oil in large skillet over medium heat. Add onion and leek, and sauté 5 to 6 minutes, or until leek is soft. Add turnips, carrot, thyme, and rosemary; cook 2 to 3 minutes more, or until carrot begins to soften.
2. Add water and stir in beans and broth. Cover, and simmer 10 minutes, or until carrots and turnips are soft. Season with salt and pepper, if desired.
3. Remove thyme sprigs from filling and discard. Pour filling into 2- or 3-qt. casserole dish. Spread Sweet Potato Topping over filling.
4. Preheat oven to 375°F. Place casserole on baking pan. Bake, uncovered, 30 minutes, or until filling is bubbly. Let stand 5 minutes before serving.

Broccoli and Shiitake Mushroom Stir Fry

Fresh and simple, this is a delicious meal with or without the flank steak.

Ingredients

1/2	lb.	flank steak (sliced 1/4 inch thick)
1	clove	garlic (minced)
1/2	cup	shiitake mushrooms (dried)
1/4	cup	black bean sauce
2	tbsp.	Chinese rice wine
1	tbsp.	arrowroot powder
2	tsp.	Chile sauce
2	tbsp.	extra virgin olive oil
2	tbsp.	ginger root (peeled and minced)
2	lb.	broccoli (cut into florets)
1/4	cup	cashews (toasted and chopped)
1	tbsp.	gluten free tamari sauce

Instructions

1. In a small bowl, mix the steak, tamari sauce and garlic and set it aside.
2. Place the mushrooms in 1 cup boiling water for 20 minutes. Drain and reserve 2/3 cup of the liquid. Toss out the mushrooms stems and slice the tops.
3. In a bowl, combine the reserved liquid from the mushrooms with the black bean sauce, Chinese wine, arrowroot powder and Chile sauce. Stir and set aside.
4. Heat 1 tbsp. olive oil in a medium skillet over medium heat. Toss in the ginger and sauté for half a minute. Add the broccoli and 1/4 cup of water, cover and cook until the broccoli is tender.
5. Stir in the black bean sauce mixture and the mushrooms, cook until the sauce is thick and bubbly. Add the cashews and mix. Set aside.
6. Heat the remaining tbsp. olive oil in the skillet over medium heat. Add the beef and stir fry until the meat is browned. Return the broccoli mixture and toss to combine.

Tenderloin Steaks with Mushroom Sauce

The combination of beef and mushrooms is always a winner. Serve it with the Black Eyed Pea Salad and a Packet of Carrots.

Ingredients

12	oz.	beef tenderloin (4 ounce steaks)
1/2	tsp.	sea salt (divided)
1/4	tsp.	pepper (divided)
1	tbsp.	extra virgin olive oil (divided)
2	clove	garlic (minced)
3	cups	mushrooms (thinly sliced)
1 1/2	tbsp.	thyme (divided)
2	tbsp.	balsamic vinegar
1	tsp.	gluten free tamari sauce

Instructions

1. Sprinkle the steaks with half of the salt and pepper. Heat 1/2 tbsp. olive oil in a nonstick skillet over medium heat. Add steaks to the pan and sauté on each side for 3 minutes or until desired doneness. Transfer the steaks to a plate.
2. Add the remaining olive oil to the pan and heat. Add the garlic and sauté for 30 seconds. Add the mushroom, 1/2 of the thyme and the remaining salt and pepper. Sauté until the mushrooms are tender.
3. Stir in the vinegar, 1 tbsp. water and tamari. Cook for about a minute or until the liquid is mostly evaporated.
4. Spoon the mushroom mixture over the steaks and sprinkle with the remaining thyme.

Chewy Pizza Dough

Add your favorite topping and make it pizza night!

Ingredients

1 tbsp. active dry yeast
1 tsp. Celtic sea salt
1/2 tsp. garlic powder
1 tbsp. extra virgin olive oil
1/2 tsp. baking soda (preferably aluminum free)
2 tbsp. coconut palm sugar
3 cup gluten free flour (1 cup white rice flour + 1 cup brown rice flour + 1 cup tapioca flour + 3/4 tsp xanthan gum)
1 1/4 cup warm water (divided)

Instructions

1. Preheat oven to 350°F.
2. In a small bowl, combine yeast and 3/4 cup warm water - about 110°. Let set for 5 minutes to activate. Sprinkle in 1 tbsp. of the coconut palm sugar a few minutes in.
3. In a separate bowl, combine gluten free flour blend, salt, baking powder and remaining 1tbsp sugar. Whisk until well combined.
4. Make a well in the dry mixture and add the yeast mixture. Add the olive oil and additional 1/2 cup warm water before stirring. Then stir it all together until well combined, using a wooden spoon.
5. Lightly coat a baking sheet or pizza stone with olive oil. Spread/flatten the dough out to the edge-less than 1/4 inch.
6. Put the pizza in the oven to pre-bake for roughly 25-30 minutes, or until it begins to look dry.
7. Remove from oven and spread generously with your favorite pizza sauce, cheese and desired toppings. Place back in oven for another 20-25 minutes, or until the crust edge looks golden brown and the toppings are warm and bubbly.
8. Cut immediately and serve.

Grilled Salad Pizza

The perfect couple! All of the healthy ingredients eliminates any guilt associated with eating pizza!

Ingredients

2	tbsp.	balsamic vinegar
1	tsp.	Dijon mustard
1	clove	garlic (minced)
3	tbsp.	extra virgin olive oil
1	cup	arugula
1	cup	romaine lettuce (sliced)
1	cup	endive (chopped)
1⁄2	cup	red onion (thinly sliced)
1		gluten free pizza crust (see Chewy Pizza Dough recipe)
2	tsp.	raw honey

Instructions

To make Vinaigrette:

1. Whisk together vinegar, honey, mustard, and garlic.
2. Whisk in oil, and season with salt and pepper, if desired. Let rest 30 minutes.

To make Pizza:

1. Brush crust with 3 Tbs. Vinaigrette.
2. Toss arugula, lettuce, endive, fennel, and onion with remaining Vinaigrette.
3. Top pizza with arugula mixture, and place under broiler 2 to 3 minutes, or until greens begin to wilt.

Thai Pizza

Absolutely delicious. Use left over chicken to create a family friendly recipe!

Ingredients

1⁄2		red bell pepper (thinly sliced)
1	tbsp.	extra virgin olive oil
1	tbsp.	organic peanut butter
2	tsp.	hot sauce (such as Sriracha)
4		chicken cutlets
2	tbsp.	rice wine vinegar
1⁄4	cup	cucumber (seeded and julienned)
1		carrot (peeled and julienned)
1	cup	bean sprouts
1⁄2	cup	cilantro (chopped)
1⁄2	cup	gluten free teriyaki sauce
1	cup	Daiya mozzarella
1		gluten free pizza crust (see Chewy Pizza Dough recipe)
2	tbsp.	gluten free tamari sauce
2	tbsp.	raw honey

Instructions

1. Preheat oven to 500°F.
2. Preheat a grill pan over medium-high heat. Combine olive oil, tamari and peanut butter with hot sauce. Use the microwave to loosen up peanut butter if it is too cold to blend into sauce, about 10 seconds.
3. Add chicken and coat evenly with mixture. Let stand 10 minutes then grill chicken cutlets 2 to 3 minutes on each side, until firm. Slice chicken into very thin strips.
4. While chicken cooks, mix honey and vinegar and add the cucumber and carrots. Turn to coat evenly.
5. Place pizza crust on pizza pan or cookie sheet. Top with teriyaki sauce - spread it around like you would pizza sauce. Top crust with Daiya, peppers, and chicken. Bake until golden and bubbly, about 15 minutes.
6. Top the hot, cooked pizza with sprouts and cilantro. Drain cucumber mixture and scatter over the pizza. If desired, serve with crushed red pepper flakes on the side.

BAKED GOODS

Healthiest Banana Bread Ever

Healthy and delicious!

Ingredients

1	cup	gluten free flour (i.e. brown rice, quinoa,)
1/2	cup	coconut flour
1 1/4	tsp.	baking powder
1/2	tsp.	baking soda
1/2	tsp.	cinnamon
2		egg whites (slightly beaten)
1	cup	banana (mashed)
1/2	cup	raw honey
1/4	cup	coconut oil
1/2	cup	walnuts (crushed)
1/2	cup	unsweetened coconut (shredded)
2	tbsp.	ground flax

Instructions

1. Preheat oven to 350°F.
2. Coat an 8x4x2 loaf pan with coconut oil and set aside.
3. Mash bananas and set aside.
4. In a medium bowl combine flours, baking powder, baking soda, cinnamon and sea salt. Set aside.
5. In a large bowl combine egg whites, banana, honey, and oil.
6. Once mixed well, add flour mixture all at one time to banana mixture. Stir until moistened.
7. Add in shredded coconut and crushed walnuts. The batter should be lumpy. Spoon mixture into pan.
8. Bake for 45 to 50 minutes.

Coconut Bars

Cut these up for a delicious snack. Kids will love these as well!

Ingredients

1/2	cup	almond butter
1/4	tsp.	vanilla liquid stevia
1/4	cup	applesauce
1/4	cup	coconut oil (melted)
1 1/2	tbsp.	ground flax seed
1/4	tsp.	Himalayan sea salt
1/4	cup	Xylitol
1/2	tsp.	baking soda
1/2	tsp.	xanthan gum
1/4	cup	dairy free carob chips or dairy free chocolate chips
1	cup	coconut (shredded)
2	tbsp.	coconut flour
1	cup	quinoa flakes

Instructions

1. Pre-heat oven to 350°F.
2. Mix the first 5 ingredients together in a large bowl.
3. Add the remaining ingredients and mix together.
4. Grease a square baking pan with coconut oil and add the mixture.
5. Bake for 15 minutes.
6. Let cool. Cut into squares and keep in the refrigerator.

Pumpkin Spice It Up Cookies

A great tasty and healthy snack to cure your munchies.

Ingredients

2	cups	almond flour
1/2	cup	coconut flour
1	cup	walnuts (chopped)
1/2	cup	coconut (shredded)
2	tbsp.	Xylitol
2	tsp.	cinnamon
1	tsp.	allspice
1	tsp.	ginger
1	tsp.	nutmeg
1	tsp.	baking soda
1	cup	organic canned pumpkin
1/2	cup	unsweetened almond milk
3		eggs (gently beaten)
1	tbsp.	lemon zest

Instructions

1. Preheat oven to 375°F.
2. Line a baking sheet with parchment paper.
3. Mix the coconut flour, walnuts, coconut, sweetener, cinnamon, allspice, ginger, nutmeg and baking soda in a bowl and set aside.
4. In another bowl, use a whisk to blend the almond milk, oil, eggs, and lemon zest.

5. Add the wet mixture to the dry mixture and fold in until mixed. If the dough is too stiff, add a few splashes of the almond milk. The dough should not be stiff but easy to fold.
6. Use a spoon to drop the mix onto the prepared cookie sheet. Make sure the cookies are flat. Bake for 20-30 minutes. The edges of the cookies should be starting to darken when they are done. Let cool on cookie sheet then gently remove and place on a rack to continue cooling.

Seed Flatbread

This is a great alternative to crackers or pita bread. Enjoy this cut up with hummus or spread with almond butter.

Ingredients

1 ½	cups	raw pumpkin seeds, ground into flour
1 ½	cups	sunflower seeds, ground into flour
1	tsp.	Himalayan sea salt
2	tbsp.	ground flax meal
6	tbsp.	boiling water
2	tsp.	extra virgin olive oil
1-2	pinches	green leaf stevia powder (optional)
1/2	tsp.	garlic powder or 1 garlic clove, minced
1	tsp.	dried basil
1	tsp.	dried parsley

Instructions

1. Preheat oven to 350° F. Grind the seeds before measuring out 1 cup flour of each to total 2 cups of flour.
2. Combine the flax seed meal and hot water and let sit for 5 minutes.
3. Combine all ingredients together in a mixing bowl. Knead the dough until everything is mixed. The dough will be very stiff. Add more pumpkin or sunflower seed flour if dough seems too wet and a little more olive oil if dough seems too dry.
4. Grease a pizza sheet and sprinkle it with coarsely ground pumpkin seeds. Pat the dough into a ball shape and place it in the middle of the cookie sheet. Beginning in the center and moving outwards, squish the dough flat with your hands. Use a rolling pin or even a drinking glass to roll out the dough.
5. Bake for 20 minutes until browned (or long longer if not cooked through). Remove from heat and enjoy as a pizza or as a flat bread with veggies.

Paleo Almond Snack Muffins

The following muffin recipes are great alternatives to the high carbohydrate, high calorie versions of muffins commonly disguised as healthy!

Ingredients

1	cup	almond butter
1	cup	sliced almonds
1	cup	pure coconut milk
2	cups	unsweetened shredded coconut
3		eggs
¼	tsp.	vanilla extract (optional)
2	Tbsp.	coconut sap or raw honey
12		paper muffin liners

Instructions

1. Preheat oven to 400°F.
2. Line a muffin tin with paper liners.
3. Combine all ingredients and pour into muffin tin.
4. Bake for 15 minutes.

Paleo Pumpkin Snack Muffins

Ingredients

1½	cups	almond flour
¾	cup	canned pumpkin (or cook and puree pumpkin yourself)
3		large eggs
1	tsp.	baking powder
1	tsp.	baking soda
½	tsp.	ground cinnamon
1½	tsp.	pumpkin pie spice
1/8	tsp.	sea salt
¼	cup	raw honey (optional)
2	tsp.	almond butter
1	tbsp.	sliced almonds

Instructions

1. Preheat oven to 350°F.
2. Coat muffin tins with coconut oil (or use paper muffin cups and add 1/2 tsp. melted coconut oil to batter).
3. Mix all ingredients (except sliced almonds) and pour evenly into tins.
4. Bake for 25 minutes on the middle rack.
5. Sprinkle almonds on top immediately after taking them out of the oven.

Paleo Blueberry Snack Muffins

Ingredients

½	cup	coconut flour, sifted
½	tsp.	baking soda
½	tsp.	Himalayan sea salt
¼	tsp.	nutmeg
½	tsp.	cinnamon
6		eggs
1/3	cup	raw honey
¼	cup	coconut oil, melted
1	tbsp.	vanilla extract
1	cup	fresh blueberries
1		lemon (zested)

Instructions

1. Preheat oven to 350°F.
2. In a small bowl, combine coconut flour, baking soda, salt, nutmeg and cinnamon.
3. In a large bowl, combine eggs, honey, oil and vanilla. Blend well with whisk.
4. Mix dry ingredients into wet, blending with a whisk.
5. Fold in blueberries and lemon zest with a spatula.
6. Pour batter evenly into a 12 cup muffin tin (greased with coconut oil or if using paper liners).
7. Bake for 15 to 20 minutes.

Almond Butter Cups

These are an absolute family favourite in our house. We always have a supply of these in our freezer for a quick treat!

Ingredients

1/3	cup	coconut oil
1/3	cup	raw carob powder
1/3	cup	almond butter

Instructions

1. Line a cookie sheet with 12 mini cupcake wrappers.
2. Mix all ingredients in a medium mixing bowl. Combine until smooth.
3. Place 1 tsp. of mixture into each cupcake wrapper. Freeze.
4. Keep in freezer in freezer proof bag and enjoy one as a treat.

Coconut Macaroons

A much healthier version of an old favourite. These are great high protein snacks.

Ingredients

4		egg whites
1 ½	cups	unsweetened rough coconut
1	tbsp.	xylitol
½	tsp.	vanilla extract

Instructions

1. Preheat oven to 350°F.
2. Add the egg whites and vanilla to a medium sized mixing bowl.
3. Beat the egg whites until they become firm and peak.
4. Once the eggs are stiff, add the coconut and stevia- fold in very gently.
5. Line a cookie sheet with parchment paper and, with a spoon, drop the mixture onto the cookie sheet.
6. Bake for 15 minutes.
7. Remove from pan and place on rack to cool.

No Bake Energy Bites

A much healthier version of a granola bar. Kids love these!

Ingredients

1	cup	gluten free quick oats
2/3	cup	coconut flakes
½	cup	organic peanut butter
½	cup	ground flax seeds
½	cup	dairy free chocolate chips
1/3	cup	raw honey
1	tbsp.	Chia seeds
1	tsp.	vanilla extract

Instructions

1. Mix all ingredients together and let sit in fridge for 30 minutes.
2. Roll into small balls about 1 inch in size.
3. Store in air tight container in fridge.
4. Enjoy one as a treat.

Coconut Biscuit Bread

This recipe has a consistency similar to corn bread or scones.

Ingredients

3/4	cup	coconut flour
1	cup	shredded coconut
1/2	tsp.	Himalayan sea salt
2	tbsp.	coconut oil (melted and slightly cooled)
½	tsp.	xylitol
5		eggs
1-2	cups	coconut milk or almond milk
1	tsp.	baking powder

Instructions

1. Preheat oven to 350°F.
2. Melt the coconut oil.
3. Whisk the eggs.
4. Add the stevia and salt and continue whisking. Keep whisking and slowly add the melted coconut oil. Slowly add the coconut milk/almond milk and keep whisking. Start with 1 cup.
5. In a separate bowl mix the flour, baking powder and shredded coconut.
6. Add the dry mixture to the liquid and stir with a wooden spoon. You will have to add more milk to get to the consistency of cake batter. This is something you need to do by eye.
7. Use a cake pan and line the bottom with parchment paper and grease the sides with coconut oil.
8. Pour the batter into the cake pan and drop the pan on the counter a few times to release any air bubbles and to even out the batter.
9. Bake for 30 to 35 minutes.
10. Let cool, take a table knife and go around the end of the pan to release the bread. Flip over to release from pan, remove parchment paper and place on cooking rack.

Apple Loaf

A slice of this with a cup of tea brings warmth and pleasure to any day!

Ingredients

2	cups	almond flour or hazelnut flour
1	cup	chopped walnuts
2	tbsp.	ground flaxseed
1	tbsp.	cinnamon
2	tsp.	baking powder
1/2	tsp	Himalayan sea salt
2	large	eggs
1	cup	unsweetened applesauce
1/2	cup	plain dairy free coconut yoghurt
1/4	cup	coconut milk

Instructions

1. Preheat oven to 350 degrees.
2. Coat a 9 x 5-inch loaf pan with coconut oil.
3. Thoroughly mix the almond flour, ground flaxseeds, cinnamon, baking powder and salt and set aside.
4. In another bowl mix the eggs, applesauce, oil and coconut milk.
5. Pour this mixture into the bowl with the dry ingredients and stir until combined. If the dough is too stiff, and a few drops of coconut milk to smooth it out.
6. Press the dough into the pan and bake for approximately 1 hour. If you insert a toothpick and it comes out clean, the loaf is done. Place on cooling rack.

Easy Muffin Mix

Whip these up for a quick snack.

Ingredients

2 1/2	cups	almond flour
1/2	tsp.	baking soda
1/2	tsp.	Himalayan sea salt
2	tsp.	Xylitol or equivalent Stevia
3		eggs
1	cup	fresh or frozen berries or chopped domestic fruit

Instructions

1. Preheat oven to 300°F.
2. Use baking cups to line a muffin tin.
3. In a bowl, mix the dry ingredients and set aside.
4. In another bowl, mix the eggs and sweetener and pour into the dry ingredients. Mix well.
5. Add the fruit and mix well.
6. Using a spoon, place the batter into the baking cups
7. Bake for 25 to 30 minutes.

Almond Biscuits

For cheesy almond biscuits add 1 cup nutritional yeast. For a sweeter version, add 1 cup berries.

Ingredients

2	cups	almond flour
3/4	tsp.	Himalayan sea salt
1		egg
1/2	cup	melted coconut oil

Instructions

1. Preheat oven to 325°F.
2. Line a cookie sheet with parchment paper.
3. Mix he dry ingredient is a bowl and set aside.
4. In another bowl, mix the eggs and melted coconut oil together. When you do this, be sure to whisk the eggs first and then gradually add the oil and you continue to whisk.
5. Scoop 2 tbsp. of dough, roll into a ball and then form into a patty.
6. Place on the cookie sheet and continue until all the dough is used. Bake for 20 minutes. Store in fridge.

Cheesy Biscuits

These are so delicious. They are similar to a cheese scone but without all of the excess carbohydrates.

Ingredients

3	cups	almond flour
1	tsp.	baking soda
1/2	tsp.	Himalayan sea salt
1/2	cup	Daiya shredded cheddar or mozza
2		small onions (finely chopped)
3		eggs
1	tsp.	Xylitol
1/4	cup	plain dairy free coconut yoghurt
1/2	cup	water

Instructions

1. Preheat oven to 325°F.
2. Line a cookie sheet with parchment paper.
3. Mix the dry ingredients in a bowl and set aside. In another bowl whisk wet ingredients.
4. Add the dry ingredients to the wet ingredients and mix well.
5. Scoop approximately 1/3 of a cup of batter and put on cookie sheet and gently flatten so that each scoop is about 2 1/2 inches in thickness. Make sure to space well between each biscuit.
6. Bake for 20 to 30 minutes, making sure that the tops are browned. Store in fridge.

Marvelous Millet Crisps

Ingredients

1 cup millet flour
1/3 cup quinoa flour
1/4 tsp. baking soda
1/3 tsp. sea salt
1 tsp. arrowroot flour
Extra millet flour for kneading
Filtered water as needed (very small amount)

Instructions

1. Preheat oven to 350°F.
2. Mix all the dry ingredients together in a large bowl.
3. Add the filtered water a little bit at a time, creating a dough consistency.
4. Sprinkle some millet flour on a counter surface and place the dough in the middle. Start kneading; add a bit of millet flour as needed to keep it from sticking.
5. Put the dough on a non-stick or coconut oil greased baking sheet and flatten with your hands to about 1/4 inch thick.
6. Bake until browned and crispy- approximately 20 minutes. If you find that it is not as crisp as you would like, put back in the oven at 200°F for another 30 minutes.

Bean and Quinoa Crackers

These are so great to have on hand. Enjoy them with hummus and raw veggies for a light lunch or snack.

Ingredients

1	cup	mung bean flour
1/3	cup	quinoa flour
1/4	tsp.	baking soda
1/8	tsp.	Himalayan sea salt
1/4	cup	millet flour for kneading
1	tbsp.	arrowroot flour
1/2	tsp.	of herbs of choice (i.e. Thyme, Basil, Oregano)

Filtered water for kneading

Instructions

1. Preheat oven to 350°F.
2. Mix all the dry ingredients in a large mixing bowl and then add the filtered water a little at a time to create a bread dough consistency.
3. Sprinkle some millet flour on a counter surface and place the dough in the middle. Start kneading, using more millet flour as required to keep from sticking.
4. Put the dough on a non-stick or coconut oil greased baking sheet and flatten with your hands to about 1/4 inch thick.
5. Bake until browned and crispy-approximately 20 minutes. If you find that it is not as crisp as you would like, put back in the oven at 200°F for another 30 minutes.

Eggless Coconut Cookie Bars

Ingredients

1/2	cup	raw almond butter
1/4	tsp.	vanilla liquid stevia
1/4	cup	organic applesauce
1/4	cup	coconut oil (melted)
1 1/2	tbsp.	ground flax seed
1/4	tsp.	Himalayan sea salt
1/4	cup	xylitol
1/2	tsp.	baking soda
½	tsp.	xanthan gum
1/4	cup	dairy free chocolate chips
1/4	cup	shredded unsweetened coconut
2	tbsp.	coconut flour
1	cup	quinoa flakes

Instructions

1. Preheat oven to 350°F.
2. Mix everything together.
3. Grease a square baking pan with coconut oil.
4. Add the mixture and bake for 15 minutes. Let it cool and keep in the refrigerator.

Eggless Lemon Bars

These are light and fluffy and a great treat for the whole family.

Ingredients

1	cup	quinoa flakes
1/3	cup	almond flour
2/3	cup	shredded unsweetened coconut (divided)
1/4	cup	melted coconut oil
½	cup	canned coconut milk
1/4	cup	fresh squeezed lemon juice
1/4	cup	xylitol

Instructions

1. Mix the quinoa, almond flour, 1/3 cup shredded coconut and melted coconut oil into a bowl.
2. Pour into a square baking pan that has been greased with coconut oil.
3. In a separate bowl combine the remaining ingredients.
4. Spoon this over the mix that is already in the baking pan. Sprinkle with remaining1/3 cup shredded unsweetened coconut and bake at 350 degrees for 20 minutes. Once cooled, place in refrigerator for 6 to 8 hours before serving.

Vegan Walnut Chip Cookies

Vegan cookies that are to please any palate.

Ingredients

1/2	cup	almond milk
1/4	tsp.	xanthan gum
1	tbsp.	ground flax
1/4	cup	xylitol
¼	tsp.	vanilla liquid stevia
1/4	tsp.	Himalayan sea salt
1	cup	raw almond butter
1/4	cup	coconut flour
1/2	cup	quinoa flakes
1/2	tsp.	baking soda
1/2	tsp.	baking powder
1/4	cup	dairy free chocolate chips
1/2	cup	chopped walnuts

Instructions

1. Preheat oven to 350°F.
2. Combine the first 4 ingredients and mix with electric beater.
3. Add in remaining ingredients and continue to beat until well combined.
4. Spoon out the mix into medium size balls and place on a cookie sheet that has been lined with parchment paper. Flatten each ball so it is quite thin.
5. Bake for 20 minutes.

Zucchini Muffins

This is a great way to get some veggies into your kids, plus they taste great!

Ingredients

2 1/2	cups	almond flour
1/3	cup	coconut oil
1/4	cup	raw honey
3	cups	grated zucchini
3		eggs (beaten)
2	tsp.	cinnamon
1/4	tsp.	Himalayan sea salt
1	tsp.	baking soda

Instructions

1. Preheat oven to 350°F.
2. In a large bowl, mix the flour oil, honey and zucchini.
3. Add the eggs, cinnamon, salt and baking soda. Mix until well incorporated.
4. Line muffin tins with paper and put in mixture.
5. Bake for 30 minutes.

About the Author

Dr Cobi Slater is a Board Certified Doctor of Natural Medicine, Registered Herbal Therapist, Registered Nutritionist and she also holds a PhD in Natural Health Sciences. Dr. Cobi is the founder of Essential Health Natural Wellness Clinic located in Maple Ridge, British Columbia, Canada.

Dr Cobi is extremely passionate about helping others heal naturally as well as empowering patients to live a life of optimal health. Dr Cobi is a regular guest on many international radio and TV health shows. She also contributes to numerous publications as a health expert and is the author of 3 health books including The Ultimate Candida Guide and Cookbook, The Ultimate Hormone Balancing Guidebook as well as The Ultimate Metabolic Plan. Dr Cobi has helped thousands of patients regain their health through lifestyle changes resulting in a freedom to enjoy life like never before!

Dr Cobi grew up in an environment with her mother ceaselessly searching for various natural remedies to heal herself from a life-threatening illness. As a witness to her mother's dedication to nurture herself back to health through the use of natural medicine therapies which did not have the many side effects of chemical drugs, Dr. Cobi recognized that one's health is not exclusive to the physical body. It became obvious that optimal health and wellbeing stem from an intimate connection between the body, mind and spirit.

Dr Cobi's inspiration to pursue a holistic approach to health and wellbeing led her to establish Essential Health Natural Wellness Clinic. Dr Cobi is dedicated to providing professional, safe and effective complementary healthcare through the use of research and evidence-based natural medicine therapies. Offering assistance for chronic disease, hormone issues, immune health, allergies, skin problems, digestive complaints, nutrition counseling and lifestyle counseling to name a few, Dr Cobi educates and empowers individuals to achieve an optimal state of health and wellbeing.

Index

A

B

C

D

E

F

G

H

J

K

L

M

N

O

P

Q

R

S

T

U

V

W

X

Y

Z

35576240R00131

Made in the USA
San Bernardino, CA
12 May 2019